DATE DUE			

IN THE DREAMLIGHT

In the Dreamlight

TWENTY-ONE ALASKAN WRITERS

Edited by

ROBERT HEDIN & DAVID STARK

Introduction by

WILLIAM STAFFORD

COPPER CANYON PRESS

Permission to reprint the stories and poems in this book is granted by the authors and, in the following cases, by the publishers of books or magazines in which the material previously appeared: MARY BARON: "Christening," "Card for My Mother's Birthday," and "Penelope at the Loom" are reprinted from *Wheat Among Bones*, Sheep Meadow Press. ANN CHANDONNET: All poems are reprinted from *Ptarmigan Valley (Poems of Alaska)*, Lightning Tree Press. RICHARD DAUENHAUER: "Russian Easter, 1981" first appeared in *Alaska Journal*. ROBERT DAVIS: "Fertility Rite" first appeared in *Orca*. JOHN HAINES: "On a Skull Carved in Crystal" first appeared in *Permafrost*. All other poems are reprinted from *News from the Glacier: Selected Poems 1960-1980*, Wesleyan University Press. "The Writer as Alaskan: Part II," is reprinted from *Living Off the Country*, University of Michigan Press. ALBERT HALEY: "The Worm" is reprinted from *Home Ground*, E. P. Dutton. ROBERT HEDIN: "Tornado" first appeared in *Poetry*. All other poems are reprinted from *Snow Country* and *At the Home-Altar*, Copper Canyon Press. LEE LEONARD: "An Evening Beside Walden Pond" first appeared in *Permafrost*. TOM LOWENSTEIN: All poems are reprinted from *The Death of Mrs. Owl*, Anvil Press. NANCY McCLEERY: All poems are reprinted from *Night Muse*, Uintah Press. DAVID McELROY: All poems are reprinted from *Making It Simple*, The Ecco Press. JOHN MORGAN: "In Which a Total Eclipse of the Moon is Eclipsed by Clouds and a White-Tailed Deer Bounds Off into the Woods," "Seasonal," and "Smoke" are reprinted from *Bone-Duster*, the Quarterly Review of Literature series. "The Bone-Duster" first appeared in *The New Yorker Magazine*. "Barnstorming" first appeared in *The Massachusetts Review*. "The Arctic Herd" first appeared in *The Black Warrior Review*. SHEILA NICKERSON: "Wiltshire in May: An Idyl" is reprinted from *Waiting for the News of Death*, Bits Press. Selections from *Songs of the Pine-Wife* are reprinted from the book published by Copper Canyon Press. RONALD SPATZ: "Kabob" first appeared in *Fiction*. "Tricks of Finding Water" first appeared in *Panache*. IRVING WARNER: "Fever" is reprinted from *In the Islands of the Four Mountains*.

The publication of this book is made possible by a grant from the Alaska Humanities Forum and the National Endowment for the Humanities.
Special thanks to Centrum, where Copper Canyon is Press-in-Residence.

Cover illustration and calligraphy by Catherine Doss.

Copper Canyon Press
P.O. Box 271
Port Townsend, WA 98368

Contents

Introduction

The world happens twice—once what we
see it as; second it legends itself
deep, the way it is.

To BREATHE along through this collection of stories and poems by Alaskan writers is to enter an enhanced world, one that we already know, and another one called forth. There is the stark, close-up world presented in an unblinking way by experienced observers who are knowing about life in the rough; they have been there and have come to tell us about it. They have the place names and the local terms and attitudes. This is one part of the collection.

There are stories and poems that weave that outer world of bush or street with another world, with echoes from shamans, and from European shamans like Carl Jung; there is an interweaving of outside culture and local commitment. This is a strong part of the collection.

And in this collection there are dream-intensities—excursions of fantasy, Gothic, or funny, or just one of those original figure-eights-in-the-head that artists can bring off.

Through this whole book runs a feeling, a realization that we all live in a time of change: a light of exploration flickers in the background of these pages. Something was, something is, and something else is trying to be. Through the cunning of the writers of an area, readers can venture into the exotic by way of the known, and come out enriched. These women in town, in the bush, these men hunting, pipe-lining, hanging around . . .— their explorations are the best for readers who are seeing and touching the same immediate world, and that other rich world unlimited except by the power of thought and imagination.

William Stafford

IN THE DREAMLIGHT

DAVID McELROY

Molt of the Winter Soul

A warm noisy family adopted me
from the mileage I used to make,
from silences I thought of
as stunted spruce standing in groups
on moonscapes along the Alcan.
Just night and more winter coming
to track the whiff of my exhaust.

I thought I'd made it.
I went south, doubled back
in snow, walked backward
in snow, dissolved my trail
south again through water.
In soft shoes I lost my smell
in Seattle and New York, New York.
It didn't work.

I've changed my skin almost,
the orphan crust sloughing off
to show a darker warmer layer.
Again tonight it is early winter
in the temperate zone of America.
My wife and children are fast asleep
in blackness, breathing easy.

My hand scratches pages in hunger,
a patchy pinto creature pawing
old snow down by the willows.
A twig snaps in the hall.
From the darkness of my son's room,
the cat studies my movements
for hours. Her frozen gold-slits,
the quiet eyes of the arctic lynx.

Up the Alcan

So ends the story of The Boy
And His Flying Machine And Dog.
I throw the book on the dash
and keep driving the pickup
in low gear, twenty miles an hour,
my throw-out-bearing shot,
a hundred miles to the next gyp
joint across the Yukon.

Sancho Panza, wonder dog,
drools on my thigh. Fat, dumb
and happy in the golden dream
of the Great Pika Rabbit Corral.
His chubby toes quiver in pursuit.
He moans wisely then yawns.
The mouth that ate the west.

I open Sister Mary Gilbert's
book across the horn
on the wheel. On the one hand
I steer. On the other, I push
the words flat against the page
so they won't bounce off
across the tundra with the bears.
This poem's about the undertow.

This road was built for war.
Curves, loops and doodles
on a flat plateau made convoys
safer from strafing that never
happened here. The chrome ram
on the hood sweeps the horizon
in a steep turn. I'm a hero
on the prowl.

Without warning the road
coils in a pile behind a tree.
Caught in the vortex,

both hands on the wheel,
the words fall down, break,
and the page comes tumbling after.
A coyote whips by.
One quick look:
the zeros in his eyes.

In Memory of Arden Davis: Smokejumper 1966

The spotter slaps our legs and we tumble
from the Doug down to sudden silence.
Bad form, the plane and then the ground
spin above me. Behind me, Arden leaves
like a fetus, perfect, a white boulder
heading home through the green air.

For a moment our bodies are all we have,
nervous circuits in space. Static lines
snap. Our chutes explode out round.
In shrouds we swing just right and dream our lives.

Eskimos stare at the same nightmare each March—
that perfect approaching peeled orange.

We fall and turn like clockwork
over tundra, trees, avoiding the Tanana
going back on itself in sine curves
S-ing to the sea with a current so certain
even geese go down. Below,
good men are stumps, bad for the ankles.

I yell at my friend. We wave our arms
like angels. We've decided. We're staying.

Puget Loons and Figure in Coat

Steep g's. Their wing tips flex concave
in tight turns where good scenes warp with weight.
They sight down on downtown smokestacks, smog,
log booms, bay, and you, the aphasic bum
on the trestle hunching home with oatmeal to the tunnel
you know but can't name. Cops call you Honest John
because you're old and jobs you pull are puny.

Light fingers, this bad weather keeps you clean.
Breaking wind, blaming spiders, you jabber
down the line becoming less. Barnstorm pilot,
the seat of your pants, baggy as a chimp's ass
in pants, still steers, and air is everywhere.
Two loons crisscross away so you see one.
The mate flies dead in parallax.

With passes east choked on snow, grain freights
stalled off schedule and barley seepage nil,
no chicken in the pot, no wonder water birds
are girls you rolled in Rio thirty years ago.
The gold gone, your last engagement flopped in Nome.
These tracks curve into the earth, vanish to a point
you're walking to, the next rock after crust.

Open barns and your wing walker passed away.
You can't fly for wages, nor dive for visions
in strong water the pulp plant makes, riding
a loon's back down, going on air your bones hold—
those Indian summers coalesced in the femur.
You lumber blind down runways of my blood.
If I blink you're off and gone light as lint.

Barbara's Cannery Ritual

The belt goes by for days
lugging sockeye to our knives.
Dressed white and horny as a nurse,
I stand all day. One foot and then
the other. The belt goes by.

One fish plus four flat strokes
make two fillets. Meat in one tub,
guts in the other. A female, I stab
her head, flop her over. Four strokes
divide bone and guts from meat.
The eggs spurt pus-yellow.
Chuck them in the gut tub.

The belt splice goes click-click
on the rollers. Toward me, by me, away
down the line of working women, all white
except for green gloves, black boots, and me
their friend. I strop my blade keen.
The belt conveys my eyes to the window
and out a chute where green swells
come to relax on the sand for days.

We chatter over machinery. My neighbor
can't laugh and isn't half as fast.
Her smock hides an ass so flat
she had to stack two pillows
to get one kid. Our talk clicks
like marbles in a bag for days.

The belt goes by for days.
When I quit this shift some say good-by.
I disappear in the woodwork
of their town, but my hands remember
the knack of strokes when I butter bread.

Mack trucks are loading canned salmon
bound for Kansas and casseroles.
Forklifts shuttle in and out.
The drivers, acting smart as horses
frisking the wind, pivot on the ramp
and slam crates down hard on the truck bed.
This Grade A meat won't show the net
bruise or pattern of the scales. Children
know white milk comes from a wax box.

Tomorrow's off. Tonight I'll do
my hair and bake a frozen pie.
I'll watch tv and plan parties where oildrums
bang with ice and beer, and clothes feel
so soft you fall asleep just wearing them.

The belt goes by.
We hose down soon.
The Tajlum was high boat
at Salmon Banks, the Tender said.
Tomorrow he's due in, running the late
tide out the Strait. He'll walk tired
up our hill, smelling of sea and diesel.
I'm in the kitchen boiling ferns
or out back bringing in the wash.

Last week I heard his fingers gallop
on the fender in the front yard a moment
before he caught me from behind
pulling panties off the damp line.

Mean Mother Metaphor

In the cold ocean only whales are warm, also walrus
in a foot of fat, and specks of birds on slate waves
bobbing in the chop.

Squid, skate, salmon, merman and maid, seaweed, all
dissolve deep in degrees of gray, wave coldly
and swim the same.

In radar light, currents click rocks through tons of oxygen
like the liquid popping of your spine. The Aleutian chain
erupts muffled

as the belch in a cow. Atomic testing beats the bony plates
of the sturgeon's head, vague as human data in my dreams
of news reports

watched alone in a blue room where I am usually smoking.
In the dumping ground cod search car seats. They signal
coldly and drive the same.

Perch stare out bus windows. The octopus fingers an ash tray.
Polyps grow on a radio, and a starfish eats a doorknob
tight as a fist.

I eat you when words don't open. Taking off your clothes
you grow blacker and fabulous, larger in the room
and in my eyes.

In my cold poems the white chemicals from your body
stick to my tongue, warm and bitter like a shiny penny
soaked in salt.

Later, I'm lucid but weaker and pumping gas for my own ambulance
before the wrecker dumps me and metal in the sea.
My splash ripples out

and in the tympanum of the killer whale sounding for the right
whale's tongue, a chunk of pulp behind baleen—sweet
as passenger pigeon.

Off Point Moler and Amchitka mad hulks breach for air,
erect and small in reported fog. The killer clings.
The tongue spurts blood

black with hemoglobin, and the right rolls fin out.

LEE LEONARD

An Evening Beside Walden Pond
or
A Yellow Truck and a Big Mac
Is a Hard Combination to Beat

THERE is this fellow I know pretty well, who at one time was paid good money by the government to ask silly questions of strangers. Well, apparently it became a habit that he can't break because one day he asked me if I knew whatever happened to Walden Pond. "Sure," I said. And then I told him this story.

*   *   *

It is evening in Fairbanks and the white neon figures on the Alaska National Bank Building bleed into the haze as they flaunt the vital signs of the day: 8:45 . . . −52°. In the Goldstream Theater parking lot, the lights have turned the snow to a ghastly fluorescent purple. But it is here, over by the chain link fence, where the row of yellow pickup trucks is parked, that Walden Pond emerges like a hotdog plucked from a pushcart kettle, out of a wavering cloud of steam. But this steam is not warm and moist. This is a steam with a difference, for at this temperature the air can't support water vapor. At this temperature all vapor turns to frozen fog, instantly. And here this ice fog billows from the tailpipes of the yellow trucks. There is no one in the trucks. They idle quietly. Together they resemble a display of Harvest Gold refrigerators, all defective and leaking gas, and out of this lethal cloud comes Walden Pond.

*   *   *

Walden glances toward the bank, wondering why the time and temperature are so important to banks, then regretting his ignorance of economics, continues on. He crosses the parking lot to take a place at the end of the long line of men which extends back from the doors of the theater. With the exception of Walden, these men look pretty much alike. They are tall and slender, wearing Stetson hats and waist-length suede jackets with sheep-skin linings. Their long tapered trousers are held at the waist by

carved leather belts, and all wear western boots. These men all belong to
the yellow trucks. The average has been running about 1.2 men per truck.
The trucks belong to Alyeska Pipeline Service Company. Alyeska, as their
press releases indicate, is the firm responsible for the design, construc-
tion, and maintenance of the Trans-Alaska Oil Pipeline. The carbon
monoxide content of the truck exhaust is about 0.8 percent by volume.
There is nothing in the Alyeska press releases that says they are responsi-
ble for air quality, and neither are its men. They are going to the movies.
They will only be responsible for Papillon and Robin Crusoe USN.

*   *   *

By now more men have filed in behind Walden Pond. They look much
like those in front. Walden is the only one destroying the continuity of the
line. He is short, and huddled in a rumpled Air Force parka, worn levis,
and battered white bunny boots, he has put an unattractive notch in the
line. It looks like this:

TTTTTTTTTTnTTTTTTTTTT

But if Walden doesn't fit, he tried not to show it. These men are loved
by the Chamber of Commerce because they take up space and spend
money. They are hated by most of the townspeople for the same reason.
But Walden stays neutral. When someone meets his glance, he nods and
smiles. He is wondering how they can stand there in such flimsy clothes at
fifty-two below. The mere thought of it chills him and he squirms deep
inside the folds of his parka. It has been nearly thirty minutes since his
ride dropped him off and already the cold has begun to prick at the seams
of his clothing like a hypodermic needle searching for the chance to suck
out a few more cc's of heat.

An interesting idea occurs to Walden. Perhaps it is possible to store heat
in the body while in the south and then have a reserve to fall back on when
you come north. But the whole thing doesn't seem likely, and he looks for
another answer, finding it in the yellow trucks. Whatever immunity
these men have against the cold, it must have something to do with the
yellow trucks.

Up front the doors are being opened and a wave of anticipation sweeps
the line. The men are preparing to move; they stiffen and suddenly
become aware of their posture. But Walden is not concerned with style,
only haste. There is a hole in the side of his left boot, and his toes have
become numb.

Style never was one of Walden's strong points. He could remember
what it was like at the air base in New Mexico; he would lie on his bunk

and stare for hours at the cool green map of Alaska, as it clung to the blistered paint on the cement block wall. He had dreamed then, of entering Fairbanks in style; of driving his dusty pickup down the main street to the riverbank where an old man would be standing in the shade of a covered boardwalk in front of a log saloon. "Just come over the highway, bub?" the old timer would ask. "Com'on in, I'll buy you a drink." And Walden would spend the rest of the afternoon in the cool darkness of the bar, listening to stories of placer mines and homesteads in the bush, getting all the dope he'd need if he was going to make it on the last frontier.

In sixty-seven Walden's dream came true, with modifications. He had a brand new pickup of his own then and on the thirteenth of August he came driving down the broken pavement between the used car lots, but there was no dust; it was raining; it had been raining for days. In vain he searched for the log saloon by the river, then settled for a converted government surplus hangar called Hell's Half Acre. He did meet an oldtimer. Her name was Rita, but she could tell him nothing. The dope she had was for sale. It took several drinks for Walden's brain to resign itself to the reality of the place, and the rest of the day and the night that followed is now just a bald spot on his memory.

By morning the rain had stopped. Walden awoke with a sense of urgency. Raising his swollen cheek from the wad of newspaper that separated him from the floor, his eyes came to focus on a cherry veneer chest of drawers. There was a message awkwardly carved into the side: THIS IS MY BODY BROKEN FOR YOU . . . REMEMBER ME. Walden got the message and jumped up, searching the room for his wallet. Through the greasy haze on the window he could see his truck in the street below. But the street was gone and in its place was a river. The men unloading the contents of the truck into a boat they had docked to the tailgate paid little attention to Walden's cries of protest, which were muffled behind the glass.

The next day Walden stood for hours in line at the insurance company claims office. The sign above the door showed a great pair of benevolent hands thrust forward with a tiny car, house, and smiling family cradled in the fleshy parts of the palm. This sign was a great comfort to Walden until it became his turn at the desk. The agent carefully explained that the flood had been an act of God, and apparently Walden's truck hadn't been insured against acts of God. He demanded to know how they could be sure a flood was an act of God. He demanded to know how they could be sure. But they were sure. They had a list. They showed it to him. Floods were number twenty-three on the list.

"Theft!" Walden countered. He knew he was insured for theft. With only the slightest indication of impatience, the man carefully explained that theft during an act of God could only be considered part of the act. "Can I get insured against acts of God?" Walden asked.

"Of course, but it will cost you a lot more than you are paying now."

The next day Walden moved in with a group of hippies who lived on a hill.

* * *

As the line brings Walden closer to the door of the theater, he looks back at the row of yellow refrigerators, wondering if the lights go on when the doors open. Alyeska trucks are supposed to have every option you can get, including the big heaters. Walden never even got to try out the heater on his sixty-seven Ford and he hadn't had a truck since. He had a sixty-two Rambler for awhile, but that wasn't the same.

* * *

Inside the theater he slides a five-dollar bill across the counter to the cashier. She is young and lovely, and Walden smiles, knowing that the braces, pimples, and dandruff are only temporary. But she stares back coldly. This is the last of his money, but she accepts it anyway, and pressing a button, she forces the counter to spit up a purple ticket. Another button spills two quarters down a small chute to a circular tray where they lie motionless. She counts out two singles: ". . . and two makes five. Thank you," she says to Walden's money. It is unsettling for him to discover that the world has reached the point when teenagers will only touch paper money. But he points this out to no one and hurries along to find a seat.

* * *

Walden has found a good seat in the center section not too close to the front. By sitting in the middle of the row he avoids the awkwardness of having to let people pass. For if he stands to allow someone by, his timing will inevitably be off and they will step on his feet. Husbands leer at him with jealous accusations as he makes room for their wives. It is a situation to be avoided whenever possible, especially tonight. Tonight Walden is celebrating. As of this date Walden has existed on earth in his present form for a score and ten years. He has kept it to himself.

In the darkness of the cartoon he slips off his boots to thaw out his toes. Only the toes in his left boot are cold. There is no real reason to take off the other one, but he loves them both equally and will not discriminate against the wounded one. After all, these boots are not surplus like so many others in Fairbanks. Walden got this pair new. He traded a switch knife to a supply sergeant for them. The knife came from Mexico. On one side of the handle was a tiny scorpion embedded in clear lucite; on the other side it said JUAREZ. On one side of each boot was a small air valve; on the other side it said DO NOT INFLATE WHILE AIRBORNE.

Continuing his preparations, he makes a nest of his parka against the back of the seat. The parka is very dear to him also. He ripped it off personally, before leaving the Aerospace Team. Walden never complains about his time in the service; the Air Force had been good to him. Training for instance: mechanic on C-130 transports, "HERCS" they called them. And travel: two years in southeast Asia. It was a good job. Walden liked the predictability of machinery, and the Herc was a predictable machine. He once sent a silk pillow to his mother with a picture of a Herc on it. The background was blue like the sky and the plane was sewn in silver thread. Below the airplane the word DhaNang was embroidered in gold. She never had mentioned how she liked it.

Walden's Air Force training started to pay off when he got to Alaska. They discovered oil on the North Slope in sixty-eight and there were lots of Hercs flying out of Fairbanks. He got a job with no sweat. He never forgot what the recruiting sergeant had told him: "Herc training is worth two years of college." He'd been right. After the work slowed down and Walden was laid off, he sat down and figured it out. If he had saved everything while he had been working he could have put himself through two years of college.

In seventy-four the pipeline work started, and the Hercs were flying again, but the freight outfits were getting their mechanics wholesale from Georgia. Walden hasn't lost heart, figures when the cold weather comes the outsiders will leave. It is now mild December.

*   *   *

When the movie begins, Walden is taken aback. He has never been able to endure realism. But he will tough it out. He can identify with Dustin Hoffman and Steve McQueen.

In the liquid heat of the South American jungle, McQueen is continually being beaten up while Hoffman gives himself hemorrhoids with a small metal tube which contains a seemingly inexhaustible supply of money and other incidentals. Walden can't help observing that, with a tube like that, Batman would never need a belt.

One scene especially amuses Walden. The prisoners are lined up receiving work assignments from a grizzled man behind a desk. Dustin Hoffman has bribed a guard to get easy jobs for himself and Steve McQueen, but something has gone wrong and they're being sent to a hard labor camp. A similar experience recently happened to Walden. Someone gave him a tip on who to see at the Alyeska personnel office. Hoping to make a good impression, he borrowed a flowered western shirt and a pair of straight levis. What luck, Walden thought, entering the office, the man at the desk was wearing the same shirt. "So you're Walden Pond."

"Yes, that's right," Walden replied, trying not to appear biased.

"And you think you can walk in here, dressed like that and pick up a free ticket into the middle class. Well, boy you ain't foolin' nobody. Look at your belt." Walden did as he was told.

"What about it?"

"I don't see no flashy buckle, no steer head, no semi truck, no Caterpillar Tractor. You think I'd miss somethin' like that?" He turned to the man at the next desk. "Look here, Rainard, this fella thinks we're gonna miss somethin' like that." The other man shook his head. "Sorry, son, but we can't use you."

In another scene Steve McQueen has escaped. He is taken in by a tribe of Indians and is sleeping with a beautiful young girl. Walden is sleeping with a beautiful young savage, too. Her name is Janet. She is from the Jackson tribe of Santa Barbara, her father is an orthodontist there. She has good straight teeth and a dirty mouth, and insists on being called Pond's woman. But there are problems. Sometime during the two years they have been together she became "Aware." Now she is totally aware, so she broods; over the condition of the ozone layer; over the direction Rock has taken in the seventies; she broods over everything. Walden isn't aware, but he can live with it. It's her nature thing that he thinks has gotten out of hand. It has reached a point where she seldom washes, and when she does she won't use soap, "chemicals" she says. No longer will she shave her body hair, finds the custom "barbaric." Yet she will brush her teeth five times a day. Walden is no longer sure whether he is in love or has a perspiration fetish. He knows he should be rid of her, but Walden lives in a cold climate and stubbornly clings to warmth whenever he finds it. More than anything else he wants to get married, but Janet would never buy it.

*   *   *

Fifteen minutes into Robin Crusoe USN, Walden's seat is empty. It has been years since he could believe in Dick Van Dyke. The frozen surface of the parking lot sucks the heat from his boots, but he pays no attention. He feels good, the feature has ended happily with Papillon floating to freedom, borne up by a raft of coconuts. He knows there is someone he should thank, but can think of no one in particular so he continues to the corner.

Walden waits at the light. Caravans of yellow trucks glide by on plumes of blue exhaust. Behind the glass, smiling faces look down at Walden. They look like pleasant, friendly people. The story goes: "Why do

Alyeska people roll up the brims of their Stetsons? So they can fit three of them in a yellow truck."

Across the street, MacDonald's parking lot is filled with yellow trucks. Icy vapors billow up around them until they seem to dissolve. There is a law in Fairbanks against idling an unattended vehicle, but Walden is a peaceful sort, he will make no arrests.

Through the glass still more lines of men are visible. Orderly and uniform, they file back from the stainless steel counter. Inside Walden takes his place at the end of a line. The girls who hurry to serve the customers are exceptionally clean, so is the floor and the tile walls. The counter itself gleams. It is Walden's turn at the counter now. Everyone is smiling as if delighted by all the cleanliness. A child with beautifully clean teeth is giving him a Big Mac, large fries, and chocolate shake. It is all packaged in a clean white paper bag. He offers her two-fifty, and she takes it, but he doesn't leave right away, he has only taken a step to the side. It is obvious to everyone but Walden that this action is causing confusion in the lines. He is trying to figure out whether to eat here or take the food home; Janet thinks Big Macs are the purest form of poison. Slowly he becomes aware of his situation. The edge has gone off the communal spirit of the place, and the mood has turned sour. At last Walden realizes that he has become a restriction, impeding the smooth flow of commerce, he knows his business is finished, he must leave.

*   *   *

In the purple dusk beneath the mercury vapor lights Walden stands clutching his white paper bag to his chest as if it were a small child. He is considering the unpleasantness of hitch-hiking home while the heat drains away from his Big Mac. It is a dissatisfying thought and his mind turns to Papillon drifting on his coconut raft in a quiet sea.

*   *   *

Moments later he is driving down Airport Way in a yellow truck. Warm air boils from the defroster vents. On the soft naugahide next to the white paper bag a coffee-brown Stetson heads south.

On the dash Walden finds Dotty West, Merle Haggard, and Buck Owens. He leaves Dotty and Buck and plugs Merle into the tape deck, the lights and the ice fog fall behind as the Hag sings of hard times and wild women. Walden feels good, relaxed and content. The power steering yields to his touch, the truck floats over the corrugated surface of the snow packed on the highway.

A few miles from town Walden pulls into a turn out at the side of the road. He climbs out of the cab and walks a few steps from the truck to relieve himself. He watches his stream cut into the snow and disappear through a ring of steam into the ground. Walden knows this place. From here a foot trail leads to a badly abused piece of ground to a small lake. At the head of the lake is a cabin. Walden can see the light in the windows flicker as Janet moves about inside.

It was while cutting a hole in the ice of the lake, some years ago that Walden heard God speak. "How you doing, Walden? Everything alright?" The sound seemed to be coming from the hole in the ice, so Walden got down on his hands and knees. A ring of cold vapor curled up around his face, but he could see nothing.

"I'm okay, I guess," Walden said to the hole, but there was no answer. Later Walden figured it had only been loneliness tampering with his imagination, but he still isn't quite sure.

Walden takes a moment to look at the cabin and the lake, remembering the voice. Then, looking back down the road, he reaches for the door of the truck. The interior light welcomes him back to the warmth of the cab and he pulls out, still heading south.

Hurtling down the white strip of highway toward the gash in the black spruce at the horizon, Walden reaches for his Big Mac. A faint reflection flashes red on the windshield in time with Merle's music, he ignores it.

*   *   *

Beyond the metered glint of red, beyond the glass, beyond the white road and the black forest, the aurora twists and bristles. It surges with quivering rhythms from one side of heaven to the other as if projected across the screen of a giant drive-in. And now, like the fade-out at the end, the white light waves then ripples, forming, just for an instant, a single word against the darkness.

PROSPERITY

MARY BARON

Card for My
Mother's Birthday

Thinking of you today   Mother,
I send my mind along road maps—
the curves shaped by New England lanes,
fat, yellow stems of interstate
the routes of old migrations, old
returns.

          We tainted whole cities
the winter gray of helplessness
the watercolor gray of hate.

Mother, your grave is along here
a road I haven't driven since
the day I turned my back, and left.
Eleven years, and I still dream
you soothe me in the night; you throw
me down the stairs.

          Mother, I've been
running away from you so long
I'm lost. I'm on a spider's road
one of the tenuous pale lines
that web where I live now, the scarred
center, the heartland of America.

Christening

Mary Margaret Josephine—
Mary after Nanny, that fierce
old lady, loved and feared, after
my mother, secondary always
who finally drank herself to death.

Margaret for Peg Kelly, Irish
milkmaid. She hung lace curtains
up against the streets of Dogtown
and told stories I believe in still.
Margaret for her one daughter, dead
from walking in the Easter rain.
The ribbons on her bonnet ran—
the color blurred, and she dissolved
and Peg told me the story.

Josephine I chose. Ugly,
they said, but I wanted St. Joe
the quiet one, the underdog.
Yosephina, the Bishop sang
and slapped me hard across the mouth.

Mary Margaret Josephine—
I used to think my real name
was Anastasia Cinderella—
today I know it is an emptiness.
I fill it with the names along the road
Black Water   Mad River   Roaring Branch
Yosephine, Soldier of Christ,
gone AWOL, somewhere in Ohio.

Penelope at the Loom

The pressure of hot blood pounds from the Hall.
As I wait here, Telemachus himself
grows old enough for lust. Odysseus
loses and finds himself, monotonous,
and I weave nothing I can keep.

*

The blond-haired boy watches me from the door.
Last night he saw my finger rip the dark,
tearing the web, unravelling
postponing time,
    I am betrayed—revived,
forced to take up my life; finish the shroud.

*

The shroud lies in the chest. Sitting in sun,
I weave the darkness of my heart. I let
the blond one watch.
    I drown Odysseus
among the cotton threads; Telemachus
I arm for war. But when the shuttle moves
around the figure of Penelope,
the dusk comes down, unravels what I see.

*

The blond one watches day and night.
What does he think of me? Why do I let
him stay? We hear the others in the Hall,
singing, alive.
    I tighten, firm the cloth,
weave in the fragments of my dreams. At dark,
I cannot sleep. I pluck the strands apart.
My mind cannot face its own face.

*

I lie down on the living bed, its post
a tree, symbol—of something. I forget.
The meanings have been gone for a long time.
Odysseus, husband, do you remember what
they are?

*

Tonight the blond boy sleeps outside
my door. Nothing my mind can shape has made
him speak or turn away. I think that I
belong to him.

He is my death, growing older along
with me, until we lie together here
upon my husband's bed, until I am
turning, twisting, reeling, full of life
unfaithful at the end.

Animus

In your house
in your absence
I feel your gestures fly to my hands
your expressions settle on my face
gently as the doves outside
landing on the wire

Though we move separately
through solitary landscapes
always
there is smooth stone under creek water
always the one
under the other's skin.

Sea Otter Woman/ Instructions

When they dim the lights
be ready—

the barred shadows across your bunk
will take my shape, blurring
over the sheet, over sea ice
then water

        When we surface
there will be nothing but

                spindrift and sea swell
wind

    men lolling like bowhead
will be breathing together
drawing in/pushing out
the great breath of the world

TOM LOWENSTEIN

Blue Dreamlight Shaman Song

In the blue dreamlight, the blue dreamlight,
    in the blue dreamlight,
        the blue.
An old man is afraid, a hunter is afraid,
    in the blue dreamlight,
        the blue.
A young woman, a young wise woman,
    in the blue dreamlight,
        in the blue.
In the blue dreamlight, blue,
    speak, crouched by water,
    in the blue dreamlight,
        the blue.
We have brown and snowy circles,
    in the blue dreamlight,
        the blue,
we have long circles under the mountains,
    in the blue.
Great mountain drinks from sky-hand,
    the blue dreamlight,
        the blue.
Great mountain drinks:
grass, rock, moss, satisfy their thirst,
    in the blue dreamlight,
        the blue.
We have chains of little families,
    in the blue dreamlight,
we have chains of sojourners and women
    in the blue dreamlight,
        in the blue dreamlight,
        in the blue.
From beginning to the end,
    blue dreamlight in the blue,

from beginning to the middle,
    blue dreamlight in the blue,
Whale, raven, bear, salmon, fox,
    in the blue dreamlight,
        in the blue.
Whale, man, gull, dog, ptarmigan,
    in the blue dreamlight,
        in the blue.
O it is now,
    and it was then,
O it is now,
    and it was then,
  in the blue dreamlight,
    in the blue dreamlight,
      the blue.

Tlingit Burial

Aj! he was carried on his back,
he was carried from the houses, past the Sitka trees,
from the corners where the women sat,
who wove the whale crest on the dance blankets,
who stitched roots and seeds to make the cooking baskets,
who twined grass, and cut the raven's feathers
to decorate men's hats.
He was carried secretly;
and young girls menstruating,
crouched in little branch-huts
gazing at the sea through pine cones,
squinting between needles, between twigs,
at the cold sky and the sea.
And new-born children lay in haggled cedar-bark,
spit bubbling their mouths,
crying out like warriors in dreams.
And grown men—with their cousins,
with their sons, their sisters' sons,
Bear Clan, Raven Clan and Whale—
sat shifting nearer to the blaze,
faces pitched, or greased, soot-painted, red with cinnabar,
and wept grieflessly, drinking mouthfuls of hot wood-smoke,
moved closer, arms and shoulders heat-raw,
passed the Raven pipe, shook the oyster catcher rattle,
turned carefully the heavy carving,
fingers curled about . . . crouched closer, suffering the heat,
where the fire roared to the blue hole,
and the fire rolled through the roof hole,
and the flame stretched like a pine tree,
and smoke rose to join the sky and cloud . . .

    And some are berry-gathering on the hills,
and some are travelling to summer fishing-camps,
following red salmon and white salmon:
others moving northward, catch the Small-fish
(and have buried their canoes in the sand,
boiling *ssag* in them for thick white oil)
        and they do not know it

(who are salmon fishing, who fill berry-baskets,
who will come home at the small moon
with dried salmon stretched on sticks)
they do not know (who fish, who pick),
he lies there with his back uncovered
in the hemlock woods, where flies touch him and mosquitoes
    pierce:
and only we, the small, have come to lift him,
have taken our direction from the sea,
(raised him from the branch-bed)
and travel along half-darkened paths,
journey where wet needles and the steepness
and the water makes the paths hard,
following the path we hear the sea from,
hear the water to the west beneath the cliffs . . .
But the path is difficult,
and we have wound back over dry rocks,
abandoning the one that has the stream-sound at its feet,
the path our feet left marks on in the spring,
we have gone back deeper in the trees,
we have walked where we can only feel the darkness,
where we hear the windy sea,
like white lights through the forest.
But him we carry, him we carry,
eyes darkened, ears deaf to sound,
to movement, to the forest speaking,
he cannot listen, does not hear our song,
our hasty breathing, as we carry him.

Nor sees the light grow,
nor feels the wind that lifts and drops his hair.
And he has left the dream of moth, wasp, bird-song and the
    whale,
the darkness of bear's head, and the tall ant-hill,
and comes now to the dream of fish, the stone under the wave,
approaches the dark and light parts of the fire, the bone, the sky.
    And we come into the light,
we come into the sea-light, cloud swaying off the sun
(and Raven flew up on the sea, against the cloud,
the salt of the grey waves blowing on the wind)
and we stand motionless, the cold air on our muscles, on our
    arms,

and in our eyes the cold air stiffening.
And we bear him, who is cold too, but not cold,
across barkless tree trunks that have scattered from inland,
we cross them murmuring,
lest the dead trees wound the dead man before burial
(before fire) . . . But we arrive on shore-rocks,
we tread them, step on sand,
and we lay him on the stones,
and we lie down with him on the sand and stones.
And he is singing a long song into the wind,
it is the water, bone and fire song,
the song of sea-wood, and the green above it,
the song of long cloud on the sun,
and the great cliffs of trees.
    And we gathered branches,
gathered wood and broke it into sticks,
and we piled his seat, high as a man's ribs, for his body.
And his song stopped, for the sea had taken it,
his song stopped, for the wind had swept it off;
and we made fire, and sang it back to him,
but in the bright light of the sun, the flames dissolved,
and the air shook in the bright light of the flame.

Then we laid him in it, and they clasped him,
then we threw him in the smoke, and it wrapped him,
and in the flame we could not see him,
not his body, not his song,
but saw the shadow of the Raven in the flame,
and he was not visible to men's eyes again.

The Carpathian Swallow

IN 1959 there was a sighting of a great Carpathian swallow, a bird of beautiful discreet colors, feathers of soft brown-greys and unusual plumgolds. The Parisian millinery wanted him; I was selected for the expedition. The man who was to take the bird had been a world famous game hunter but was getting on. I was told he was 84 that year. I saw him first at the Paris customs, a slender figure in a soft yellow hat, with a face which struck me as tragic. The bones were good, but the skin tracked over as if by little bird feet, the eyes a depth of vivid amber, a surly nose. His slacks did not fit him properly about the hips but hung awry, like sacking.

"My last expedition," he said in the limousine.

"But sir,"

"No, no, I can accept my limitations. I'm old." He turned his face to me and I saw a challenge in his eye. A silence. "I'm old," he said again.

"Weathered, sir, but not old," I told him finally. He showed me the base of his left thumb, a ring of teeth marks, also old.

"My wound," he said. His lips stretched open and his gums appeared. "Find another."

"Sir?"

"Go on, find another. I dare you."

I looked him over. There were creases, soft agings in his skin, mottled from tannings on the vast African plains, a puckering on his upper arm. I pointed a finger and raised my eyebrows. He cackled.

"No, no! Small pox vaccination, 1941!"

"I see I was wrong," I smiled at him.

"You don't know," he leaned close to me and I saw strange, electric sparkings in his eyes, "how wrong you were."

I inclined my head. He settled back into the cushions and closed his eyes contentedly. I felt as though, somehow, I had primed him for the hunt.

I didn't see him again until we had actually assembled at the base of the mountains some days later. Rumania was wonderful that hour, I remember, bathed in a particular kind of sunlight which softened her stony outlines. There was a wind from the sea, salt and dead jellyfish, whalespray and old song. That kind of air. The Explorer was standing at the sloping base of the mountain we were to ascend. He was gazing upwards through binoculars. I went to stand beside him and requested the binoculars.

"Sorry," he said. "Prescription, you know." His guns all had prescription sightings, too, I was to learn. But he admitted it in such a frank manner, with no sign of self-pity, that I felt none for him. We were to begin on horses, and I rode beside him up the gently winding, then steeply rising path. There were small yellow flowers on either side, and I watched the hooves fall among them, smooth and powerful. I was struck by the Explorer's boyish form as he sat on his horse. From the rear he had the delicate lines of an adolescent boy. His hair? A wave in the wind, the yellow-grey of old hair.

Shortly after lunch his horse threw him, and he narrowly escaped being crushed by its rolling side. But he sprang up! As I tightened his stirrups for him he looked down at me and again I saw the strange charging particles in his eyes. He smiled the smile which pulled his lips from his gums.

"My bones," he whispered, "are made of rubber."

"I'm inclined to believe you sir," I said. "You had a lucky escape, there." He extended his little finger toward me.

"Break it," he said. "Go on, I dare you! Try!" Between my own fingers it had the slippery, flimsy weight of an old finger. I felt that I could snap it and crack the air with its breaking, like a new bean.

"I feel its resiliency, sir," I said. Just then came the whistle to move forward. Ahead of us the mules and packhorses began their slow plod. Local men in large, broadbrim hats rode first, followed by a string of lean guides, and the local priest. We were flanked by the photographers and the press. We wound up into the thin air, a dark undulant thread upon the mountain side. Rumania spread out below us, so far down that we could see the movement of clouds across her plains, blowing wildly, scudding like breakers. In the shifting light our horses seemed the only solidity. Dusk came and we camped in the shadow of an outcropping of rock. The Explorer's tent was set away from the group, and late that evening I saw him, still sitting before his fire, a hunched, slim figure. He turned his head towards me; I stood and walked over to him.

"Did you need anything?" I asked softly.

"Do you know this bird?" he asked. I crouched beside him. Our voices were whispers of smoky air in the dim firelight.

"The swallow?" I said. He nodded his heavy head.

"I've seen pictures, sir, beautiful bird."

"Is it a predator?" he asked, in an indifferent tone, looking away from me.

"I don't believe so," I told him. "Grains and wild grasses, a few insects,

a small toad or perhaps a mouse, maybe a squirrel occasionally or some-
thing larger, fox, small sheep. But no, not instinctually a predator, sir."

He nodded. Then, "And is it a quick bird?"

"How do you mean?"

"Is it alert, or vicious? Is it defensive?"

"I would suppose, sir, that given provocation—" He interrupted me.

"I am quick."

"I've seen that."

"Do you want to know," he said slowly and distinctly, turning his head
from side to side, "just how quick I am?"

"I believe you, sir," I told him. "So help me, I do. Marvelous, how
nimble you are."

"Run!" he whispered. "I'll catch you!"

Spoken in the dark, with only the gusting red of the fire for light, those
words gave me a chill in my pelvic region that I have never felt since. I
remained beside him for a few seconds, then sprang to my feet. Quick as
an animal, he was on me, clinging around my neck with his long,
unbreakable arms. His knees gripped my ribs. Gasping, I shook him off.

"Quick, ay?" he said exultingly. "Quick as the bird, d'you think?"

"He won't stand a chance," I said. "Not with you, sir."

Two more days saw us reaching the summit. There in the crags the
Carpathian swallow made his summer home. We were vigilant, camping
all around the summit for three days. Hour after hour we watched in the
chill, depleted airs of that mountain top for the rush of bright wings, the
shadows, the beating air, that would signal the roosting swallow. The
Explorer behaved curiously. He refused to take protection for himself
against the bird, and would sit with his khaki shirt unbuttoned, his
drooping chest exposed to the sandy winds. At length I was instructed by
the guides to ask him if he weren't cold, upon which he removed his shirt
altogether and dared me to find a shivering place on his body. After that,
we left him alone. He sat out on a crag with his long, glistening gun,
scanning the skies.

The bird approached on a Thursday evening, wheeling down from some
great height, uncautious and surprised when the gun discharged and blew
off a portion of his tailfeathers. These, plummeting straight to earth, were
quickly collected and lugged to a dolly, where they were preserved in a
nonacid treated paper wrap. In the setting sun they seemed fantastic trees,
tropical and brilliant. In the meantime, I had run up to the Explorer.

"What happened, sir? Gun misfire?" The bird still in sight, and there
was no time to be lost.

"The new models," he said, with a great dignity, "are those which
must be braced. I was unable to brace mine."

"Allow me!" I cried, and went before him on all fours, giving him the flat of my back. I glanced upwards between his legs and saw a grim, triumphant expression on his face as he waited for his shot. His skin had yellowed to the color of his eyes and he seemed to blend with the ochre rocks around him. Only the slow, particular pulse in the wrinkles of his throat gave him animation. He was a frozen, crouching figure, tireless. I felt rather like a dog. We waited.

The shot! It catapulted me forward, over the cliff edge. I grabbed for the shrubbery and clung weakly to some roots. Feathers speared the air, bronze and lilac, wicked to the flesh. Men threw themselves upon the earth. I saw the priest raise his hands. And I alone, dangling from the roots of a sturdy Carpathian pine, was protected enough to raise my head. There on the summit, the Explorer wrestled the swallow, who had landed, critically wounded, bereft of plumage, angrily territorial. The naked skin of the great bird was so leathery, so yellow in hue, that at times it seemed the Explorer and the bird had merged into some half-beast, buffeted by the scouring summit winds.

Now the Explorer had gained the advantage, leaping onto the bird's back, pummeling it with his fists. Now he was down, and the swallow was preparing to rake him with its talon. But no—the man wrested the talon away, overturning the bird, falling upon its iron throat. The swallow made an effort and threw him over. Yet the bird was tiring; the caws it unleashed upon the air were feebler and fewer in number. The pendulous swing of its great head was labored, and as I watched, the beak fell off with a clang as it hit some rocks. The body folded. After some moments the Explorer rose to his feet. He swayed once and began to stagger towards the rest of the party.

"Sir," I croaked to him as he passed, his boots on the level of my head, "Sir, could you be so kind—"

"Who's there?" he said.

"Your assistant," I said feebly; my strength was going. I kicked my legs into the vast space beneath me. "Sir, below you, to the right."

He looked down at me, sweating and an awful color.

"What the devil do you want of me now!" he cried. "Haven't I proved to you, to all of you, enough today? Haven't I had him?"

"Sir, you were a marvel. But sir"—he had turned away—"Sir, for the love of God! Holy Jesus!"

"What is it you want?" he roared. His eyes were terrible to see, with the minute snappings of tarnished light making them the only vital elements in his body. "Haven't I given enough?"

"Your hand, sir," I gasped to him, and loosed my left hand from the trunk of the tree; it bore deep impressions of bark and was almost numb. I extended it, trembling, toward him. He bent and grasped it with his right, shook it briefly, and turned to look over his shoulder, where cameras were being assembled. I heard a cheer and he bowed several times. In the sky to the East aircraft were breasting the crags. I could hear the distinctive chop of a Rumanian helicopter, and I became desperate—suppose he could be distracted?

"Sir!"

"Enough, dammit!" he said. "Leave me in peace. Haven't I—"

"Sir," I felt myself weakening, "I don't believe you're as strong as you once were."

"What? What's that you say." He turned back toward me.

"That's right," I gasped. It was painful to breathe. "I think you're failing sir. I think the bird has finished you. I think if I slipped down here one more half-inch you would no longer be able to pull me up. I think—"

"I dare you to try!" he said, bending down close to my face; his lips slid away from his gums. "I dare you to slip down that half-inch there," he cackled. "Make it an inch, two inches. Come on!"

Slowly, I let myself drift towards the great space below. One arm remained clamped around the roots where they merged into the trunk. I moved it ever so slightly. A jerk—his contorted face next to mine, veins straining against the skin, a smell as of things singeing—my collar rose and choked me. I tumbled forward and landed in a sandy depression some feet away. He staggered to me.

"What? What?" he gasped. I coughed for some minutes.

"Sir," I whispered, "you're not old." He stood over me, gloating as if I were the Carpathian swallow, and demanded his tribute.

"What's that you say? Ay?" His eyes were embers in his suffused face.

Pam Before Morning

DURING the summer when the man in the next county was arrested for committing an unnatural act with his spotted horse, I fell in love. She had lived for many years in the town with her father, but never seemed to age; her two clean front teeth rested upon the cushion of her lower lip even when her chipmunk face was quiet, and her eyebrows—mobile, winged—were like a small girl's. Her body was thin and breastless, but there was her name, Pam, short for nothing but her whole, uncluttered self, Pam Updegraff, who fastened blue plastic butterflies into the hairfall above her ears.

There was a rally that night in our town to talk over the situation in the next county. In the broad street people milled or sat on curbs, listening to the speaker. The speaker was appalled by the recent discovery. We must, he said, look closely at our neighbors. Did they have several pets? Did their children play with our children? And what of the horse in question? Should it be allowed to graze openly in its field, which unfortunately fell on the county line in full view of State Route 83? School buses passed by daily. Such an animal could only be considered an abomination in the eyes of God and man. A committee was formed. I saw my ex-wife getting involved, so I strayed away.

In the gusting of the torches I noticed her sitting on the hood of my Ford pickup. Her eyes were as big and dark as plums and she was clutching at some material bunched at her waist. She had always been around but only then I seemed to notice her. I came up from behind and slipped my hands around the corded stalk of her throat. She gagged and clawed wildly for a moment, before she heard me laughing.

"Hey, Pam."

"Real cute, Brodie. I almost peed myself."

"You really interested in what's going on here?"

"I'd think. It's not far from here, you know. The field where it happened, I mean."

"That old horse don't have a hell of a long time left."

"Listen, Brodie, I think," she said, biting her lower lip, "I think it would be wrong to kill that horse. He was, well, used."

She turned her face away as she said this. It was common knowledge that in our senior years of high school one of Pam Updegraff's father's friends had paid to court to her for three months. What he wanted, and got, were two acres of storefront property on Layton Street. During those three months Pam was more firefly than human; she wore a low cut ill-fitting pink dress that draped around her high white collar bone, and she was always jiggling her toes, hanging on the man's arm. But all that was years ago, before my ex-wife and I ever were engaged.

"Brodie," Pam was saying, "you don't think, well, that it was the horse's . . . well, the horse's wish."

"No . . . but what's there to do about it now? You want to take a ride out to the Casa Loma?" I always would take them to the Casa Loma first. My ex-wife's brother was a bouncer out there and he had it set up for me. I could walk in, snap my fingers, and the drinks would arrive on a green felt tray. I wanted to see Pam's small hands close around one of those tall, cool glasses. I wanted to help her forget that I was the guy who had set the table cloth on fire at the senior prom, roasting peanuts in the candle. But she didn't want to go out to the Casa Loma. What she wanted was to go out to the field and steal the horse away before something was done about him. I said, no way. But she kept looking at me.

We had to crawl under barbed wire, and worst of all there was a clear night sky. We were silhouetted for a mile on either side. The horse was lying down in the very center of the field, with its ears back. Grass dripped from its jaws. Pam ran her hand down the stubble of the close-cropped mane. She whispered, "It feels so funny to be petting a horse, who, well, who—"

"Get out of the way, God dammit," I told her. I put the rope over its neck and it rose to its feet, a great dark shape, like the prow of a ship breasting a wave. Pam led it across the field and through the gate into the woods. I watched her pick away, wincing as she stumbled and dropped to her knees now and then. The horse waited for her, shifting from foot to foot, snorting into the damp air. Right then my feeling came through for her. It was that she was so determined, somehow.

We had to push against the horse's withers as he clopped up the boards into the truck, and the moon showed the deep pied red of his moving flank. Pam's arms were taut, her head hanging between them as she shoved. She followed the horse into the shadows. Her voice came muffled, "I'll ride with him."

I sat in the cab trying to figure out why all of a sudden she had gotten to me. About half way there she knocked on the connecting window and I pulled over to the side. She climbed out of the back, a strange thin figure in the red lights.

"I'm cold," she said. She rode in the cab with me the rest of the way, huddled in the far corner from me, her head leaning against the window. We let the horse out fifty miles away, in the north of the state. Pam leaned forward to the window a long time to watch him as he stood in the strange field, alone, but already eating an ear of new, milk-white corn. She was silent all the way back, except once she said, "I liked to have died when you set that tablecloth on fire. Remember that?"

"No," I said. I could see her smile in the dim light, the way she gathered her lower lip under her teeth and tilted her chin. And in the driveway of the Updegraff house—an old French mansion scrolled and heavy with cornice and lattice, railings vinecrusted and risky, a yard clumped with a dying elm—in the driveway at 3 a.m. Pam Updegraff gave me her mouth in a dumb, untutored kiss, squeezing my jowls between cool palms.

"Thanks a bunch, Brodie," and hopping from the cab, she ran a few steps toward the porch, then pivoted suddenly. Her face, with its perky, gifted slantings, popped back into the window, "Thank you for a very nice evening," she said in a flat voice, bobbing her head, and then darted away again, as though that stale mannerism was no real part of her, but a leftover from the days when she sat in the porch swing with her father's friend.

I never was with her again, though I tried and tried. I called her a few times, but she was never there. And I drove past slowly in my Ford, so maybe she would look up from the garden where she worked in the evenings, barefoot in a pair of iron grey dungarees, the only color the blue or yellow barrettes clipped up over her temples. But it seemed to be too late for her, and even in August, when they burned the barn in the field where it happened, she stayed away.

JOHN MORGAN

Seasonal

My neighbor's painted flock
of plywood geese, his polished boots

sit on the stoop; inside
the trigger on his gun drips with grease.

The days shorten like dresses,
like pants rolled over the knee.

Everyone plugs his car in and darns mittens.
The sky   the sky   the sky

as wide as that, a cold blue sail,
at night it loops metallic lights.

The wolves have eaten my neighbor's dog,
its bones in a ditch seen in a dream.

Fireweed spills a last blood-petal,
the long silence leaves its mountain and sets out.

The Bone-Duster

Two adolescent summers
wasting in the basement
of the Peabody Museum
   the dampness from stones
rising along my arms, sleeveless as I dusted
the bones of
a thousand extinct pigs: it seems
I have written about this before,
moving down the stacks from drawer
to drawer, seems I
will always be writing the poems
that might have soothed me
then. Then as now
the smell of damp stones, of
bones, of wood aging in basements and slow dust,
pieces of tedium drifting down
and down on the calm air.

           and then up to lunch
     in the bright fluorescent
hall of birds, table on
table lined with limp bodies, sparrows and weavers,
auks, hawks, and puffins, all typed, all
labeled, gold, red, green, and brown-feathered lumps
laid out behind us as we ate.

          Again
I toss my lunch bag
into the bin, again the slow freight
elevator, dim and rusting,
lowers me down and down.

In Which a Total Eclipse of the Moon Is Eclipsed by Clouds and a White-Tailed Deer Bounds off into the Woods

Friend, I give you this consolation:
our losses die with us.
               It was
only last week or last year
you had imagined a clear deep pool
where jewel-like fishes sat
in perfect understanding. Only the rain
disturbed their clarity, but when you returned to the spot
it was not the same: it was yourself
in whom that rich and tragic place
called up the need to back away and stare
on emptiness, dusky, elusive,
and somehow hostile to the whole you sought,
a whole which continued to vanish
as you crept up lasso in hand. Trepidatious.

   Frankly, the night is much too shifty for us,
but if there is an answer
perhaps the children have seen it glancingly from their windows
during a moment's silence in their secret play
as a cloud flits across the copper moon
and the white tail of a deer
flashes beyond the summer-house and disappears into the woods.

Smoke

Behind the house of a friend
the earth fell away in sumac and weeds,
and there, beneath the butcher's
meat rack, the cigar store, the barber,
in the ghost of a station
on the old Putnam line, defunct,
doors ripped off, booths and benches
carted away, we'd
leap from the platform,
race up the flaking concrete steps

and leap again. There
in the men's room's hovering dark
while our mothers went shopping
above us, we'd pull down our jeans,
piss on spiders and worms,
and then run home. On the mantel
a blue plaster angel, one
wing broken—what
he had to do with that sunken archive
where I leaped into my own?

Later—it was Amalfi—I was twelve,
and on the saint's day,
as we watched from the cliffside hotel,
rockets and flares blew past
and a luminous cream-coated band from Monte
Carlo lit into Beethoven's Fifth:
oh, all that brassy fire!
Next morning mother was sick, father
obtuse, embarrassed, asked
if I knew the word 'menstruation. . . ?'

Was it then I first thought of the pool
and the colored fish? That I'd
grow up so soon, become myself
a father, teacher of what I don't know,

and what I was meant to be
shoved aside, until
this hand on my shoulder—is it anger?—
what shadowy thing? as though
it was fire I'd believed in all along,
the darkness within me gradually filling with smoke.

Barnstorming

Winter keeps us inside. My wife
tells me she is terrified
of death: how everything vanishes
and nothing you do can change this.
Then today, warm weather. In a
friend's four-seater, we fly
north to Rampart, a village
on the Yukon, a ghostly airstrip, cabins,

dark chips against the snow;
banking, heading south along the
pipeline, I ask for the controls
and find my fear of the ground
taking us higher, up
to cloud-level, where, in luminous mist
I yield, easing us back toward
rolling ridges of spruce, thousands
of black-barbed brush-strokes on white paper.

Suddenly Jeffrey leaps from his seat:
"Hey . . . *Hey!*"—knowing first flight.
At home again I say the shape a
life can take can make the end
less terrible. She says the
thought of dying brings a shock
to her body so bad she can't
sustain it, if you could hold

it steady in your mind you'd go mad.

The Arctic Herd

Together we stare at the map,
a land so vast whole herds can
vanish; each lake a lung. Angry,
he is my father and my other

self: his face comes forward
with its three days' stubble.
By night, the differences are harsh
layers of cloth between us. We

sit in the darkened cabin, pass
a jug, and put the stain of
wine upon our lips. Thirty years
a wife and son are missing;

how fragile my disinterest
in such matters. Caribou—come
dissonant reports from
far-off valleys. Cartridges and

thunder. We men without holdings
have to follow over the blue-
and orange-flowered tundra, crossing
borders, urgent into what future?

At dawn on a farther ridge they
reappear in thousands like a mist
whose eyes sprout crystal
lichen, small buds and blooms of whiteness.

That night I dream; between his ribs,
translucent like stretched rawhide,
the heart too is a map. A scar-line
like barbed wire rides across

one nipple. He stands beside
his tethered dogs. The herd's dry
bones excite a fine white
ash above his moss-packed roof.

h Time

Each time
I visit you
it gets harder
to sit next to you
my hands want to
touchtouchtouch

I want you
like owls want eyes

Silhouettes in Flight

The sea otter
weaves
her silky fur
with the sinew of her spirit's
strength, the owl

Together
they soar towards freedom
open spaces
two silhouettes in flight

The Worm

A YEAR after the accident Walt got the call. The company man said Walt was a good hand, must be tough, kid, to come back from whiplashing iron ready to hit her again. The accident was over and done, one of those things. Walt said yes, he was tough. He wanted to go on Platform Hood first thing in the morning. He wanted to give the Inlet a go again and give her hell.

Walt took from the cabin closet the barracks bag that held his gear and hard hat. He carried the bag over his shoulder on the path around the lake. The wind was punching the spruce tops back and forth, and clouds were moving in. Bad Peninsula weather came with long clouds. The girl saw Walt with the bag and behind her cabin window waved. She vanished from sight. Walt ran as fast as he could under the weight of the bag. Already she would be touching the bottles, taking wine from the shelf.

They kept the light on in the afternoon and Walt kicked his boots off and drank warm wine, chilled wine, then cold white wine that was as cold and clear as the best. He talked to her about going and making a lot of money, coming back, going and making more money, love going to be easier now. They finished talking. During the night she rubbed his back and she said Walt was knit like new, it hadn't even been a year since the accident, had it?

"It was a year several days ago," Walt said. "Twelve days, to be exact." His scar was a long surgical one across the kidney area. She rubbed the scar and Walt said the skin there felt to him like a smoothed weld. The girl said she would remember how the scar felt when he wasn't there. Walt said, "It will only be two weeks. Then we'll have a solid week together before I have to go back."

"But only," she said.

They slept touching and unmoving. Walt's stomach was pressed flat. It was hard as wood from sit-ups, vee-ups, leg lifts, and paddling a canoe. His arm muscles were tight from lifting dumbbells and swinging the ax in back of his cabin. He was twenty-two years old. They got fogged in during the night.

It was everywhere in the morning, thick and drifting away but still too thick to see piss past an arm's length. Cold, Walt waited for the chopper to show at the West Shore facility. He had a headache he could not clear except with coffee, and there was none there. The other men stood on the gravel pad or sat on their gear, smoking and talking about the latest weather rumor. The rumors came up the hill, passed on from guys at the bottom sitting in the pickups with heat and radios going. The latest was that the toolpusher on Platform Bruce told the *Husky*'s skipper that the Inlet was socked in from Homer to Turnagain Arm. A mechanic said it looked like the sky was going to squat on them for a few days and there would be no choppers going on or off anybody's oil platform. He threw his cigarette to the ground.

Walt walked to a storage shed and put his back against the plywood wall. He began to become very familiar with his wine headache, until he picked up the chopper beat. The bird was three minutes away, over the water, and getting closer and louder. With the fog they did not see the chopper until the rotor wash kicked up dust and bent the trees around the perimeter of the pad. The turbine whined as it settled to the ground and the pilot let the blades spin down.

"No more ghost-riding for this boy," he said and jumped off the pontoon. Some of the men moved close and said, "What do you mean?" The pilot said he meant the sky, she didn't love him. He sang it for them, a tune he had made up. The fog had rolled shut just as he saw the point.

"I'm lucky I'm not still out there chasing my tail," the pilot said and he started down the hill singing, "She don't love me." Walt shouldered his bag and walked from the heliport to the pickups. The fog got thicker as they drove to Rigtender's Dock. Walt saw it lying in all the low and hollow spots.

On the tug Walt filled himself with warm coffee. He took another cup onto the foredeck. The engines picked up and Walt smelled diesel mixed with salt air. The dirty and fresh air opened his nose as the tug pulled into the fog and the choppy Cook Inlet water. Walt looked over the side and saw grey, silty water. The deckhand came up and said Walt looked like hell.

"I thought you were being sick there," the hand said. Walt leaned on the rail. The hand leaned on the rail. His whiskers were wet and close to Walt's face.

"I'm not sick yet."

"Come here, kid. Do you know about the suicide basket? That's how you're going up to the rig from the boat. You stand on it, hold on, and the crane lifts you eight stories."

"I know about it." Walt moved over to the bow.

"The suicide basket may make you sicker than you are. Boy, I've seen big men lose their little old breakfast halfway up. There's all of God's sewer, the Inlet, below, and above you just a tiny, swinging cable. I don't recommend it if you're afraid of heights."

"I'm not afraid of anything," Walt said. "And I don't feel good."

He turned and faced the pilothouse so the spray and air hit the back of his neck. The flag on the pilothouse showed in the fog sometimes, flapping fast. Walt's hair was blowing. The hand could not get behind him and stood outlined in front of Walt, chewing, hands in pouch pocket.

"A man got killed out here last week," the hand said. "You know, on Hood."

The hand did not know the complete story. He knew nobody else had been hurt and there was one stiff at the end of the day. At Rigtender's they had heard the ambulance hauling ass to the heliport, and the chopper came in from the Inlet low and fast like a jet. They didn't hear the wagon go back because it did not need to run the siren. It had a stiff.

"That's tough," Walt said.

"Here we is," the hand said and pointed behind Walt. The oil platform's flare showed at one hundred yards. The flame curled, rolled, twisted yellow-orange with a blue halo. The gas burned the only hole of light in the fog.

"I bet we hit her today," the hand said. "Watch the postage stamp, by God."

The tug closed on a leg of the platform. The leg was twenty-five feet in diameter and it got bigger and the water was foaming around it. They heard yelling inside the pilothouse, then the boat turned hard and tried to back.

"Didn't I tell you?" the hand said.

Her side scraped hollow metal and the tug shuddered. Walt slipped. He looked up from the wet deck and saw the derrick lights way above and the red aircraft beacon winking on top. Walt got up bitching about banging his knee. The hand was still standing, playing with a coiled line.

"You're lucky, boy," he said. "If you fall over into the drink, you'll be dead inside four minutes. Your pockets and creases fill with Inlet mud, your muscles go numb from the cold, and that's all she wrote." The crane on the platform lowered the suicide basket. The hand told Walt to take her easy and think pleasant thoughts. The basket was coming down.

"I'll think what I want," Walt said.

Walt stepped off the suicide basket onto the metal deck. He heard the drill pipe banging in the derrick. Then the rig engines took off sounding like they always did, as if they were about to blow up. The bullcook came out of the barracks unit and down the stairs.

"Welcome to Platform Hood, the third-class postage stamp of Cook

Inlet," he shouted on the way down. The bullcook was a dark, big-belly kid with short hair and a white T-shirt. "We feature the scarf and barf kitchen and the have-it-your-way custom john." The bullcook took Walt's bag up the stairs. "You look sick, even for here. Did the suicide basket bother you?" he asked, then, "Haven't I seen you before? Weren't you on Charlee?"

"Someone else," Walt said.

"I'm Jerry the Bear. Prowlin' and a-growlin' and sniffin' the air." Jerry put a finger on one side of his nose and sniffed. "You'd remember me."

"I wasn't on that rig," Walt said, remembering well. "You're real funny."

"Maybe you weren't there long." They went inside and Jerry said Walt had to walk down the hall toward the cigar pollution. The toolpusher's office was on the left, and it was okay to wake him up if he was asleep in the chair, but you had to watch out for the hunting knife. And Jerry said, "No joke, I've seen you before."

The toolpusher was behind his desk with a plastic, bound notebook open in front of him. He had two toy figures sitting on the desk. They were made out of welding rod, and spray-painted gloss black. One was a stick man and one was a stick woman. The rod was twisted into two circles for her tits. Walt pulled out his yellow dispatch, but the man did not take it.

"If you're not a roughneck," Dink said, "get back on that tug. I don't want any worms. I ordered a roughneck this time." The office smelled old from many cigars. Walt was reading the name "Dink" of the plastic hard hat the red-faced man wore.

"I worked on the floor twenty weeks last job," Walt said. "I've been a derrickman, too."

"A kid got killed last week," Dink said. He swiveled his chair one way then the other then came to face Walt. The sounds of the rig engines going fast and slow were muffled in this room. "Did you hear about it?"

Walt said he had heard a little.

"He was a worm and it was his second week on the job when he went over from roustabouting to the floor. The second day as roughneck he gets it. So they say that we put him up there before he was ready. But the accident was due to his personal carelessness. Now I have the union, company, lawyers all on my neck. I got reamed out this morning because of these bags."

Dink stood up and kicked two nylon duffel bags stacked against the wall. The name Lonnie Ross was felt-marked on the sides in big capital letters.

"The parents are screaming to have them shipped to Arkansas. Do me a favor and tell that loud-mouthed bullcook to get these on the boat. You go on in an hour so get some chow now. Where's your dispatch? Don't hit my lady, her paint flakes."

Walt gave him the paper. "What position am I working on the floor?"

Dink waved his hand and signed the dispatch. "They'll tell you," he said. "You better work safely. Are you worried?"

"No," Walt said.

Jerry the Bear was mopping the hallway and told Walt that his bed was in room number ten. He had just changed the sheets on the bed. Walt told Jerry about some bags in Dink's office.

"Whose bags?"

"The dead worm's."

Jerry stopped mopping and blocked Walt's way by turning his belly sideways. Walt's headache had moved to the other side of his head and he could not get by Jerry without pushing him.

"Whose?"

"Lonnie Ross."

"That's not what you said."

Walt said, "So."

"I'm going to remember you," Jerry said. His pupils were BB size. "I see you, but I can't get you back in the picture. I seen your face and it was different and I can't remember how and when."

"You don't know me, but if you aren't too stoned I'm telling you about that dead kid's bags."

"Cool it," Jerry said and he kept blocking the way.

"Why?"

"Go on." Jerry turned and started mopping again.

"Gee thanks," Walt said and stepped carefully on the wet floor so he wouldn't slip.

"I'll get it back," Jerry said when Walt was down the hall. "I'll remember you. Sooner or later."

In the mess hall Walt went down the food line and put a steak and a spoonful of peas on his plate. The messhall was quiet except for the fans over the kitchen grill and one fluorescent tube that was buzzing. One man was sitting in the mess hall, an old guy. He had his head over his plate, and he held his fork backward, and shoveled what he ate, or else stabbed at it. Walt sat at the last table. The old guy was bald on top. He wore a cowboy shirt with the sleeves rolled to the elbows. His forearms were dark and large, but his hands were small. When he raised his head he saw Walt and the wrinkles crossed his face.

The eyes held. Walt stopped chewing and he just looked and the old guy looked back and they both must have been hearing the buzzing light. Walt did not laugh out of it, he did not eat, he waited for the old guy to move.

On his plate the old guy had a steak and peas and French fries and mushrooms. In a bowl he had green salad. He had garlic bread on the tray. He had a small plate with a slice of pumpkin pie. Walt still saw the two eyes looking directly at him.

The old guy put the fork down and said loud enough to be heard across two tables, "Let's go outside."

"What are you talking about?" Walt said.

"Let's go out and do it. You want a fight, don't you?"

"No, I don't want anything."

"What are you staring at?"

"I'm staring at nothing."

"You said the wrong thing there, son. Don't you stare at me."

Walt pointed at his plate. "I was looking where I wanted and then you start looking at me from across the room. What's wrong with you guys?"

The old guy took a swallow from his paper cup. "What did you say? I didn't hear. Why don't you just let off smart-mouthing me?"

"I'm saying what I want," Walt said. "Give it any name you like."

"You're a smart mouth." He started eating again. "Are you the new floorhand?"

Walt said, "Yeh." He had to tell the guy the last place he'd worked, except Walt did not say Charlee Platform, where the accident had been. He said the rig before that, Rig Twenty-seven. Walt had to yell for the guy to hear him. The deaf guy knew old guys who Walt must have known over at Rig Twenty-seven. Yes, Walt remembered them. They were the same old bunch of drunk roughnecks who ran the movie after dinner every night, and spilled ice cream down their fronts and all over the floor.

"Did those guys ever talk about Smokey?" the old guy asked.

"Who's he?"

"Listen, son," Smokey said. "Those are good old boys that went over to Twenty-seven. They got a sense of humor and they know their jobs. And you're a smart mouth." Walt said, "Sure."

Walt took his tray to the dish station. He heard Smokey's fork click against his teeth as he ate. Walt was trying to get out the door.

"See you on the floor," Smokey said. Walt turned and nodded. Smokey spit an ice cube on his tray and stared into his plate.

There was dried mud on the floor and there were muddy work clothes lying on benches in the change room. The locker doors were open and made the room even more crowded. A picture was taped to each door, all the pictures torn from the same magazine so that the sex job ran in sequence. The crew was standing, sitting, bending, getting into their work duds. A big fat guy moved out of Walt's way when he came through the door. Smokey was in the middle of the room. He did not have any hair on his legs.

"Who's this kid?" a tall guy with a red beard asked Smokey, who was pulling up the pants.

"What's it look like, Newly? The new worm," Smokey said.

"I told you I'm a roughneck," Walt said.

"You mean floorhand," Smokey said.

"Shut up, old man." The big fat guy put his hard hat on and it just missed touching the ceiling. He shook Walt's hand. "Welcome to the screw crew," Fred Steers, the driller, said. Fred had a scar on his face that ran from a corner of his mouth to under his jaw. The scar looked like a run of pink ice cream on Fred's face.

Fred introduced his crew. Smokey was a floorhand. The tall guy, Newly, would go back to worming and probably hide like before and take two hours to mix a gallon of paint. Brian, the other floorhand, was not there yet.

"I think Brian is still in the rack," Fred said.

"Someone wake that kid," Smokey said. "He hibernates. He ain't going to be worth beans the first two hours up there."

Fred kept going. Their derrickman was the Eskimo, Oscar.

"Do you like my pictures?" Oscar asked, but before Walt could say anything to the short native he said that once he had dropped a three-inch bolt out of the derrick. It hit a man down on the floor, broke his hat in two.

"After he got hit by the bolt he turned into a nut," Oscar said and laughed real hard.

"Don't listen to his jokes, Walt," Fred said. Newly laughed then.

Smokey had his pants on. He sat down by Walt, who so far had his boots and the coveralls laid out.

"You ever roustabout, son?" Smokey wanted to know.

Walt said, "No. I was really born on the floor with my hand on a tong." Fred, Newly, and Oscar laughed.

"Seems to me if you roustabouted as recently as last year," Smokey said, "then that makes you nothing more than a worm with a little floor experience." Smokey took out a can and put some snuff under his lip. "I told Dink we needed a regular floorhand on this crew, some age and experience, but they keep sending us more punk worms."

"Sure, let them send more hemorrhoids like you, Smoke," Fred said. "Everyone will be on Jerry the Bear's custom toilets all day and we'll never get below two thousand feet."

"Say, that's funny, Smokey, old boy," Walt said and nudged Smokey with his elbow. Smokey did not laugh. Then Brian came.

His eyes were still closed and his hair was pushed to one side and the hair stuck out in back and on one side. Fred introduced. Walt had his regular shirt off and his back to the wall. Walt saw Brian looking at his arm muscles, then lower.

"Where did you get that scar? That's a mean scar."

"Where did you get the long nose?"

Fred looked at Walt's scar, Newly looked, and Smokey looked. Walt put on a T-shirt slowly.

"You're right man," Brian said. "I'm sorry." Walt said "Okay." "No hard feelings?" Brian asked. Walt said "Okay." Brian yawned and sat down on the other side of Walt.

"Well, I hope we bust ass instead of sit ass today. I've got to wake up."

"You better hope for a breather after yesterday," Smokey said. "Two and a half round trips."

"I like round trips," Brian said. "It gives you something to do, in the hole, out of the hole, count the stands, one-oh-nine, one-ten, that's nice."

"Screw thee," Smokey said.

"That's the idea, Brian said. "In and out, in and out with the screw crew."

Oscar asked if Walt liked the picture on the locker. He asked Walt what he'd do with the girl in the picture and how he'd do it.

"I'd do it as often as possible with some of me down and most of me up," Walt said. The crew laughed. They looked where Walt's scar was hidden under his shirt.

"Are you a badass in town?" Newly asked.

"I'm bad wherever my ass is at," Walt said. He had the coveralls on and was standing around. He threw his hard hat at a locker. The headache had vanished. Walt got the hat back and told a story about busting a guy with a wine bottle less than twelve hours before and going to bed with his old lady and barely stopping in time to get to the dock. Walt coated the lie thick because he felt the crew looking.

"That's why all the men hate me and the women love me," Walt said. "You ask around Soldatna."

"You know, you're all right," Brian said.

"Sounds to me like we got us another one," Smokey said.

"Another what?" Fred said and stopped leaning against a locker. Smokey did not say. Everyone got quiet.

"Do you know we had an oh-jay-eye last week?" Smokey said to Walt.

"Oh-jay-eye, hell. It wasn't an on-the-job injury, it was an on-the-job death," Fred said.

"He died at the hospital," Smokey said.

"On the helicopter," Newly said.

"It doesn't make any difference," Brian said. "He died because of the job."

"He was critically, fatally injured on the job site," Smokey said.

"He's dead, that kid is," Fred said. "That's the first guy I've lost on a crew of mine. I'm talking about fifteen years and no one never got killed."

"He wasn't on the floor," Brian said. "It can't count because you didn't have anything to do with it."

"Anyone want to tell what happened?" Walt asked.

Smokey told. No one saw it, but when they found the worm they found this here and that there. They knew. He told it just the way it happened.

On Sunday there was no fog. There was even blue sky. Out on the postage stamp the crew was in T-shirts and the sun made gold waves on the Inlet all the way to West Shore. Brian and Lonnie Ross, working on the west-side catwalk, caught the best of the afternoon's sun and they'd pulled their hard hats down to shade the eyes. Lonnie stripped off his T-shirt.

"If I go down to Arkansas tanner than when I left for Alaska, the folks won't believe it. They'll put a picture in our damn paper. They put pictures in that town paper of every no-tits girl who bakes a cake. It's time they had one of me." Lonnie bit his lip, flexed his biceps, and sucked his stomach back. Brian picked up the hose with two hands. It was thick hose made with steel wire loops and quarter-inch rubber.

"Want to use those pretty muscles," Brian said.

Below a boat was tied up. The hose ran from the boat to the pump room. They were taking in cement. The hose was five-inch, heavy-duty. It kept clogging.

"Give me that thing," Lonnie said.

Brian and Lonnie took the hose apart and Brian connected an air hose and tied everything down with rope to the catwalk. They yelled at Newly inside the pump room to pressure up and they blew the line clear.

"I want to get a thirty-six from Smokey," Brian said. "Can you handle this?"

"Do you think I'm some turkey?" Lonnie said. "I'll handle it. If this bastard stops one more time that Newly's going to get shoved down it. But if this keeps running I can stretch out here and catch me a nap. Watch me soak up some of this pitiful, better-than-nothing, Alaskan sun."

"Don't tell me about the Arkansas sun," Brian said. "It's the same one."

"That shows what you turkeys up here know," Lonnie said. "You get a pissant temperature and you say, 'Oh, I'm so hot.' I'll tell you what's hot."

Brian was gone, the cement stopped pumping. Lonnie beat the metal straps on the fitting with the sledge. He broke the connection. He was looking around at the gulls that circled the back of the rig where every day Jerry the Bear put the kitchen garbage on a pallet. They were making noise and Lonnie whistled and said, "Turkey birds." Lonnie had the air hose ready and yelled so Newly could hear.

"Air, turkey."

In the pump room Newly kicked the engine on. The needle rose on the gauge, then it fell. It fell in one motion so Newly stared at zero. Then he heard something banging outside on the metal wall of the pump room, the hose.

Brian had the thirty-six-inch pipe wrench and he saw the hose dripping cement into the inlet and Lonnie Ross lying face down on the catwalk. He thought the guy was fooling except it was so quiet.

When Brian got down the steps and Lonnie did not move, Brian yelled for Smokey. Smokey saw the worm. That was the end of the story for the worm.

"The hose wasn't tied down," Smokey said in the change room. "When that connection broke apart she snaked back and got the worm right in the forehead."

"Ouch," Walt said.

"Ouch is right," Fred said.

"It was his fault," Smokey said. "The worm was playing around. That's what happens when you play around on this goddamn job."

Brian leaned across Walt to yell at Smokey. "He was a hard worker. He was trying to make an impression and carry his weight from the start, old man. He forgot to tie down. He forgot."

"Listen, son," Smokey said.

"Well, he didn't deserve what he got," Fred said. "I ain't seen a man in the oil patch yet that's bad enough to deserve it." He stamped mud off his boots and walked out.

"He learned the hard way," Oscar said and winked. "A man has got to hang on to his hose." Newly and he laughed. Then the crew went up the steps to the doghouse and the floor.

They were going into the hole and Smokey started explaining. "You'll stab pipe," Smokey said. Walt and he were hanging around the stands of pipe racked on end to where Oscar crouched on his monkeyboard high in the derrick.

"Station yourself here, see, take her, bring her over. I guide the pin into the box."

"I know that, Smokey," Walt said.

"The kids knows," Fred said. "He ain't a worm."

"Don't use your feet to set the slips. Hold them like this and slide them in."

"I know." Walt walked over and helped Brian put some new teeth on the lead tong.

"You think you know," Smokey said. He spit and went into the doghouse and got gloves. Fred said "Snap to," stepped to the stocks, and started them in the hole.

Smokey said things, shouting, but Walt could not hear over the engines. The pipe made a sprong noise and rattled as Oscar moved it in the derrick. Then Oscar snapped the elevators shut, and Fred let the clutch out and lifted the pipe. Walt swung the pipe quickly to Smokey. Smokey stopped yelling, said "Damn bitch," planted his feet, and stabbed the pipe into the pipe already in the hole.

"Don't fight iron. Make the iron work for you," Walt heard Smokey say just before the engine yanked on the tongs and made the quick air-blast sound. Then the engines revved to drop the pipe in the hole and carry the elevators back to Oscar, and with the noise none of them could have heard even the world's loudest scream. Walt hugged the next pipe and Smokey shook his head, but Walt brought the pipe dead center over the box. He stabbed it before Smokey could lay on a finger.

"Nothing to it, old-timer." Walt's back was straight and had no pain. His kidney was safe inside. All muscles were stretching out and holding to bone. Walt remembered everything.

"Way to hump," Brian, on the other tong, said.

"You're working for nothing," Smokey said the next time Walt flew in with a pipe. "Iron will swing by itself."

"I'm working for fun," Walt said. They were running the stands in fast and Walt felt the rhythm coming back. He got on his toes, pushed, swung, stood back, held, bent down, lifted back, waited, did it again. Fred increased speed and Walt laughed. Brian said they had a crew.

After two hours Newly came from the motor room and started relieving them for five-minute smoke breaks. Brian went out, came back; Smokey went, Walt waited. Already Walt's adrenalin and sugar energy was slacking off. His right arm muscle was bunching and twisting into rope. They ran the stands down and Walt worked with slow, stored muscle power that hurt. Newly was grinning.

"Where did that old man go? I'm stuck on the floor and I should be back in the mud room by now." But Newly was obviously having fun throwing the chain.

Brian called for Smokey. Fred kept them going and Smokey did not show. After they put in ten more stands he came out of the doghouse. Walt smelled whiskey right away when Smokey walked up to him.

"Now I'm going to say something and you're going to listen," Smokey said. His whiskey mouth was open and his teeth were two plates.

"You tell me what you're doing with this goddamn pipe. I seen what you're doing. You got no sense. Do you want this?" Smokey stuck a hand with a glove in front of Walt's face. He shook his hand and the middle finger of the glove jiggled by itself. It jiggled because there was no finger inside the glove.

"You think it's my own stupid fault, son, and you're right. But I learned. One second you've got the pipe wrong and everything's over, you're just looking at what was. Your finger is off 'fore the pain even starts. Or maybe you'll get your arm crushed. You're going to smash or cut all your fingers off and the pipe, she'll swing free and take us with you. Damn you, go ahead, show me your way."

"You're kidding." Walt crossed his arms. He was standing on the mat board and looked down at Smokey.

"You're screwing up again, aren't you? Show me your way."

"What do you mean, 'again'?" Walt uncrossed his arms. He had them ready. He turned his gloves into fists. "What did you say about 'again'?"

"I ain't going to watch you all fucking day," Smokey said. He pushed Walt away and tripped on the mat board, fell against the pipe. He got back and put his hand on a pipe. Then he showed Walt how.

Brian and Newly had gone to the doghouse for coffee and they were smiling in the doorway. Walt looked up while Smokey carried on about safety, and he saw Oscar way above lean over and drop something out of the derrick. The belt landed behind Smokey, but he kept talking and demonstrating how to do it with his hands on the pipe. Walt looked for Fred. He was sitting on a chain guard and his face was straight.

"Okay, all right," Walt said.

Smokey turned back to his tong and Walt whipped his glove off and shot the finger when Smokey wasn't looking. Brian laughed and came back. He said, "A good finger's worth its weight in gold, ain't it, Walt?"

Smokey said for both worm kids to take it easy, to go slower because the pay was always the same, and they had ten hours to go. He did not see Brian still laughing.

The tower ended with Walt's arm in bad shape, but his back seemed to be okay. The right arm was numb and weak so he could not make any more fists with his hand. Walt had dried mud on his coveralls, his face, in his hair. Basically he felt like a piece of mud. Smokey caught Walt before he got down the doghouse steps. "I want to show you something."

"You don't have anything to show me," Walt said and kept walking.

Smokey put his hand on Walt's shoulder. "Son, I know you don't like me riding you. I did a job on you, but I did it for your own good. A man's got to work right or else everybody gets hurt up there. If I yell at you, it's because it makes a deeper impression on you. That's psychology. You may think the old guy is a jerk, but every time you touch pipe after that you think twice."

"Is that all you got to say?" Walt said and walked out from under Smokey's hand, but Smokey said he wanted to show Walt something that would take a minute, then he was going to tell Walt something.

Smokey led Walt through the motor room, down the stairs to the pump room. They ducked under red pipes and went out on a catwalk. Walt leaned on the rail and looked at the derrick lights hitting the water around the platform leg. It was night, but it must have been still foggy because Walt could not spot the orange gas flares of any of the other Inlet platforms.

"You had a rough first day. They don't come much worse than wet pipe and mud. Whenever we make two and a half trips I feel it in my legs, too."

Walt picked some dried mud off his hard hat and dropped the mud over. His arm did not hurt so now. He was holding it loosely. "I've had harder days."

Smokey said, "This is where the worm got it. You're standing on it."

"I figured that out," Walt said.

"The worm was a dumb punk. From the time he came on, all we heard was him blowing at the mouth about how much money he was going to make, how he liked to make round trips with the pipe to build up muscles, his wife going to love his muscles and him going to use them, the best-looking girl, crap."

"Maybe he had things together."

"The worm was a teen-age punk. Too bad he ain't around, since he loved the postage stamp right down to the grease-slop chow," Smokey said. "This here old boy's got a bellyache and I'm counting my days. I've been in the oil patch since I was sixteen, but I've had enough of being stuck out here on the water on one of these stamps. The food is greasier than what we drill out of the Inlet. I got a two-inch foam mattress and you just try to sleep on that mattress. At Salt Crick, Wyoming, we used to drive to town every evening after the tower was over. Hell, I got laid every night in a good bed. I had a Chivee that was the best damn car until this bitch made off with it. I had her waxed as black as a horse's eye socket. That was the only time in my life I ever quit a job, I tell you."

"Is that what you've got to tell me?"

"You listen to me, son. After I quit you better believe I didn't have a dime or else I gave it away. That woman, she got nothing out of the divorce except my Chivee. The bitch. I ain't seen her. But I'm not talking about it. I'm just telling you that I made up my mind on tower today. This time I am getting out of this son-of-a-bitch. Old Smokey won't be coming back after this hitch."

"Suit yourself."

"The stamp just smells. It stinks," Smokey said. "Smell it. Go ahead, smell the stink. These dumb guys."

Walt asked Smokey for a cigarette. Smokey lit himself one too.

"Another thing," he said. "The doctor says my hearing is shot to hell."

"Yeh," Walt said. "Maybe you should retire, like you say. Maybe you're afraid you'll get hurt now. How old are you?"

Smokey shook his head. He said the worm had been about eighteen and married, too. Smokey said it was the girl he felt sorry for. The worm had told the story that they had driven from Arkansas to Oklahoma one night and been married because they weren't legal in their state. No one knew and she went back to living with her parents and going to high school like nothing had happened. When the worm had money they were going to get a house.

"Tell me, what's a girl like that going to do?" Smokey said. "It'll be just getting laid from now on, you just know. Don't laugh. I know girls like that, young ones. They never have the damn thing again. All you kids, these ignorant, dumb guys who get themselves killed."

"I don't see how you know about it," Walt said. "And you were talking about your health, not the worm. Can't you hear?"

"I hear you fine. I'm not talking about nobody's health."

Then Walt said it. "Did you hear about the guy on Charlee Platform last year?" He looked at Smokey's hands on the rail. They stayed the same as before, loose with the cigarette burning an orange point. Smokey spit down at the water.

"No. What about him?"

"You didn't?"

"No. I don't kid you. What about the guy?"

"Nothing. An old guy got his hand wrapped in the chain, that's all."

"See, them finger accidents happen all the time," Smokey said. Then he started talking about how last week's accident was right here, and he knew the worm had gotten it good, bought the farm, because he turned him to see the face and saw the eyes, and you could always tell with eyes.

Walt left the catwalk, stepped over pipes, came out of the pump room, started up the stairs to the barracks. He heard the rig coming out of the hole. Smokey was following him.

"Come by the room for a drink," Smokey said. "Celebrate your first day on the floor."

"You already had a drink," Walt said and kept on climbing.

"It's all right. You come by the room and have a drink. I'm next door. A man should have a snort after his first day on the floor."

"It's not my first day," Walt said.

In his room Walt finished unpacking his bag. He did not eat dinner because he was tired. Every muscle was tired. His stomach did not feel anything close to hunger. Walt sat on the bed and figured how much money he would make in two weeks. It was hard to hold the pen because of sore fingers. Walt kept multiplying the weeks until he felt rich. Then he saw the wall.

There were numbers and words written or cut in with knives on the eight-inch paneling. There was a multiplication problem—eighty-four hours times the wage. The math was all right. Walt took out his pen and put *W.C.* on the wall. He pushed the pen so it cut into wood.

Walt was in bed when Brian came in, walking lightly. Brian turned on the light over his bed and Walt said "Hello" so Brian stopped being quiet. He turned his tape recorder on loud. Someone banged on the wall next to Walt's ear. Brian lowered the volume and turned up the bass.

"Smokey's next door," Brian said and began undressing. Walt heard a loud voice talking behind the wall. "Jerry the Bear," Brian said.

"That was funny when Smokey yelled at me today," Walt said. "I felt like a turkey."

"Smokey's a good hand," Brian said and got in bed, turned out the light but let the music go. "He's an old lady sometimes. Sometimes his attitude ain't so good. Just tell him to go get laid next time and he'll be okay."

"He told me he's quitting."

"Did he say that again? He says that every hitch." Brian asked Walt if he wanted a smoke then. Walt did not because he thought it would make him too tired the next day so Brian had the smoke in the dark and listened until the music shut itself off.

"My arms feel funny," Walt said. "They tingle like they're going to sleep."

"I've had that after I took some time off last year. Your muscles are getting back in shape."

"I thought I was in better shape. I've been lifting weights for a few months now." Walt stopped.

"He was in good shape. Boy, he was strong."

"The worm?" Walt asked.

"Lonnie, right. He said hay bucking did it, but I think he got muscles in a gym. He had cans of protein, vitamins, wheat germ. He talked about the fights he was in. I guess down there in Arkansas all they do is get wrecked, chase around with beer in their pickups, and whomp each other. He was a braggadocious guy. Him and Jerry were a team. They got wrecked and dropped gin bottles from the derrick, or else when they were high they wrestled or played pool. Lonnie bragged about personal stuff you'd never believe."

"His girl."

"Especially her. The first time they went out she was cherry and she let him because a guy told him in advance everything to do with virgins, like a book of rules. Then Lonnie would turn around and tell you how she was his wife, a good church girl, ha. This here was good smoke."

Walt was glad he didn't know this worm. He sounded like a punk. Brian said, "Yeh, but he was just a kid, and what could you expect?" Brian went to sleep and Walt turned in bed and felt his muscles. They weren't so bad after a hard day. The trouble was on the outside more than the inside and the kidney. Walt could not sleep.

Walt laid on his side and rubbed low on his back over the scar. The scar always felt shiny new. Walt started rubbing the wall with the back of his hand. The pain was not too bad. Walt felt the wall and turned his hand over. He traced the letters that were scratched into the wall.

There was noise in Smokey's room. Walt heard through the wall as if it was not there. Someone banged a trash can and fell to the floor on both knees. Then Walt heard ice in a bucket of water and bedsprings. Walt traced the wall. He had one spot and he did it five times and came up each time with *L.R.*

Walt got out of Lonnie Ross's bed with its stiff, clean sheet and with his back pain. Brian was sucking in and snoring while Walt put on his pants.

No one answered the knock on Smokey's door. Walt opened the door an inch and saw light. When Walt walked into the room Smokey did not get up. He was lying on his bed snoring with his head rolled over and his arms at his side. His boots were on. Walt took a drink from Smokey's bottle and the whiskey was warm and thick. Then Walt walked down the hall.

In the recreation room Jerry said, "I'm stoned to the bone. I can play good when I'm stoned to the bone. I can really see the balls, man." Jerry kept a cigarette in his mouth and stroked a straight line. He looked up from his stick after each shot to watch the ball he pocketed. Walt said he had to have somewhere else to sleep, man.

"No prob," Jerry said and did not ask any more. "There's a softer bed in the first-aid room. There's aspirin there, too." They were walking down the hall. "I finally remembered you," Jerry the Bear said. Walt walked with the weight on the good side, pain on the other. "It was a flash," Jerry said. "Smokey was bitching tonight and I wasn't listening and I suddenly got it. You're the one they flew off Charlee last year. It was a big accident and I saw you get carried out on a stretcher."

"Somebody else," Walt said.

"Have it your way," Jerry said. He opened the door to the first-aid room. "Sleep here any time, kid. Just don't get in the bed or I'll have to change the sheets. New meat, clean sheets is our motto."

Walt felt the mattress once. "It's softer. I got sore muscles."

"Listen. Smokey remembered all about the accident after he got another drink in him. He has a buddy who was a driller on Charlee and told him. Smokey doesn't think you'll pan out on this crew. He's superstitious about guys who do dumb things and get themselves hurt. We don't want anyone else to get killed around here. My friend got killed. Do you hear me?" Jerry leaned in the doorway. His eyes were BB eyes.

The chopper pilot said, "It's a beautiful morning" and sang it to his own tune, loudly because he had the headphones on and couldn't hear himself. Walt put on a life vest, buckled in, and saw through the Plexiglas the sun coming up, the clouds down Inlet turning pink and orange. There was glare on the water as the chopper vibrated from side to side then lifted off the platform.

The platform got smaller until it looked like a postage stamp floating on smooth water. They went straight up then slid toward shore. The platform could still be seen. The gas flare burned in a straight line and it stood out crisp in the quiet dawn. The platform was smaller than a stamp.

"Is this a little emergency leave?" the pilot asked Walt and took his headphones off. "Did you suddenly get the hots for the old lady today?"

Walt kept his back straight with the weight even on both sides even though both sides did not feel exactly the same. The pain on one side burned like hell down low. Hood could still barely be seen if he remembered to open his eyes and look for it. If he watched everything closely every second, Walt would be safe. If he forgot for one second he got hurt. If Walt looked out the chopper in time the platform would be about the size of a period.

ANN CHANDONNET

Grizzly

To conquer nature is to commit suicide
    —THE FRISCO KID, Jerry Kamstra

The baby won't go to anyone but me.
But he went to the zookeeper, rode on his shoulders,
went behind the fence with him, almost nose to nose
with the blonde grizzly.

"Watch this," said the grinning keeper (who had
just been wrestling Binky, the polar bear).
He crouched and hopped.
The blonde, all 700 half-grown pounds,
crouched and hopped.
They hopped in sync the length of the cagefront;
then turned, repeated.

Back home I said to the baby
(building up his memory cells),
"Remember the bear?"
He crouched and hopped for answer.
His coat rippled in the wind like wild oats,
wild oats.

In the Cranberry Gardens

Life can only be understood backwards;
but it must be lived forwards.
                              —Sören Kierkegaard

In dense forest—
yet within sight of the garage roof—
we pick low bush cranberries
in what Yves, the three-year-old, calls "little gardens":
pockets walled in by blowdown, alders,
rosa acicularis, rank willow.
Mosses and berries make a terrarium
of one stump's hollow top.

Fall is breaking into blossom:
the gold of devil's-club and birch,
the maroon of cranberries,
the salmon and peach and flame of currant
and fireweed.
I step up onto a fallen tree.
Rotten, it descends under my weight.
Despite the heavy baby on my back,
one foot in the air, and two pails of
berries, my balance holds.
The elevator stops.
"Basement!" I step off onto moss.

In a thicket we come upon a grey boulder
with two logs fallen against it;
with a skin roof, we have shelter.
Yves takes up residence, bedding on a hummock,
breathing loudly to simulate sleep.
Here is another time: following moose trails,
picking berries, soaked lichens and brush wetting
the skins laced to my feet, twisted sinew taming my hair.
Raspberries leached white by rain
fall before I can catch them.
Currant leaves strike their flints against sodden spruce

I move forward because I must live forward,
but I rest backward.
The baby's head lolls forward onto my shoulder,
and a blue ski pole nodding in a bramble reminds me
that the fish oil rising in my throat is
capsule, not cod.

But back in the living room, when I take off my hat,
a grey moth spirals to the ceiling.

Ptarmigan Valley

Gargoyles frightened men toward heaven;
pitchy devils on ladders leered and
brandished dripping pitchforks.
In Ptarmigan Valley,
my ghost (light as the mallard feather on
Mirror Lake) floats aloft,
skimming the sprucetops like a fisher,
and comes to rest in a rose bush,
top-heavy among the airy fireweed.

Up the mountain,
in the six-foot grass,
the she-bear suckers her twins,
while her mate mumbles over a
chaw of stiff moosehide
under a cottonwood half a mile away,
scattering hair in a huge circle.

So quiet. The burner under the tea water
is mistaken for a woodpecker,
and the water pump sounds like
Doomsday.
The crisp muttering
of the birch logs on the fire,
the clock on the mantel,
coyotes howling in the foothills,
my neck chafing my collar,
my pen scratching,
these are the only sounds of this September night.

No devils here.
Perfection nudges me heavenward.

ROBERT HEDIN

The Snow Country

Up on Verstovia the snow country is silent tonight.
I can see it from our window,
A white sea whose tide flattens over the darkness.
This is where the animals must go—
The old foxes, the bears too slow to catch
The fall run of salmon, even the salmon themselves—
All brought together in the snow country of Verstovia.
This must be where the ravens turn to geese,
The weasels to wolves, where the rabbits turn to owls.
I wonder if birds even nest on that floating sea,
What hunters have forgotten their trails and sunk out of sight.
I wonder if the snow country is green underneath,
If there are forests and paths
And cabins with wood-burning stoves.
Or does it move down silently gyrating forever,
Glistening with the bones of animals and trappers,
Eggs that are cold and turning to stones.
I wonder if I should turn, tap and even wake you.

Sitka Spruce

1.

I swear these trees come from before,
Dumb stragglers from the edge.
In their trunks the fossil worm still sings.
In the shade of each branch
There are crickets still barking like sea lions.
Legends tell of main veins shooting
Deep into the earth
To feed off pools of red lava,
That some run south along the fault lines,
Churning through coastal bays and inlets—
And when a Latin peasant clears his land
The cutting and crackling of roots
Is felt here, far north
Where a tree will shiver and shed one cone.

2.

My wife and I watch the orphan trunks
Ride with the tides back to the land.
They roll and slide like whales,
Their smooth brown backs flashing in the sun.
We have seen them drifting in the Bering,
Following the songs of seals—
Uncut totems beautifully round and faceless,
Waiting for the masks of ancient clans
To rise, and chant again like the winds
That draw the foam from the sea.

3.

I have heard that when we die
These spruce will take and mother the moon.
We will find it nestled among the roots,
In a crowd of friends,
A child with a quarter face.
Stepping forward it will offer us
A gift wrapped in moss—
A pale cone out of which we pick up the sharpest teeth,
And opening our hands we prick our palms,
And watch as the first seeds of blood
Trickle and combine into pools,
Rich seas the roots curl and slide for.

Waiting for Trains
at Col d'Aubisque

4 a.m. and rain since dark, rain dropping
From the slate roofs onto the stone walkway,
And all of us here—
The middle-aged mother and the child,
The three privates smoking
As only those going off
For good can smoke—
All of us standing at these windows,
Except the young boy out under the archway
Who has brought his father's coffin
Down out of these bare hills,
A small sheepherder's boy
Who doesn't care how old the night gets
Or how long this rain takes hold,
Only that his wool coat
Is folded neatly, and that his head rests
Over his father's shoulder,
For if this boy, this young dark-eyed Basque
From Col d'Aubisque
Whose skin will never again feel as wet
Or as wanted as it is
By all this rain,
If this small boy would talk
He would say we've stood all night
At these windows for nothing,
And that even if the morning comes
And we step out into the cold light,
Finding the world no better or worse
And ourselves still wanting
To be filled with its presence,
The words we've waited all night to say
We will have to turn into breath
And use to warm our hands.

The Wreck of
the Great Northern

Where the Great Northern plunged in
The river boiled with light, and we all stood
In the tall grass staring at a tangle
Of track, and four orange coaches
And one Pullman lying under the current,
Turning the current clear. We stood staring
As though it had been there all along
And was suddenly thrust up out of the weeds
That night as a blessing, as a long sleek hallway
Dropping off into fields we'd never seen,
Into the pastures of some great god
Who sent back our steers too heavy to move,
All bloated and with green seaweed strung down
Their horns. And we all looked down
Into the lit cars at businessmen
And wives, already back to breathing water,
And saw in the cold clear tanks of the Pullman
A small child the size of my son, a porter's
White jacket, a nylon floating gracefully
Like an eel.
                          What the train and the river
Were saying, no one could understand.
We just stood there, breathing what was left
Of the night. How still the cars were,
How sleek, shimmering through the undertow.
And I saw the trees around us blossomed out,
The wind had come back and was blowing
Through the tall empty grass, through the high
Grain fields, the wind was rattling
The dry husks of corn.

Houdini

There is a river under this poem.
It flows blue and icy
And carries these lines down the page.
Somewhere beneath its surface
Lying chained to the silt
Tricky Harry holds his breath
And slowly files
His fingernails into moons.
He wonders who still waits at the dock
If the breasts of those young girls
Have developed since he sank.
He thinks of his parents
Of listening to the tumblers
Of his mother's womb
Of escaping upward out of puberty
Out of the pupils in his father's eyes
And those hot Wisconsin fields.
He dreams of escaping from this poem
Of cracking the combinations
To his own body
And those warm young safes
Of every girl on the dock.
Jiggling his chains
Harry scares a carp that circles
And nibbles at his feet.
He feels the blue rush of the current
Sweeping across his body
Stripping his chains of their rust
Until each link softens
And glows like a tiny eel.
And Tricky Harry decides to ascend.
He slips with the water through his chains
And moving upward
Climbing over and over his own air bubbles
He waves to the fish
To his chains glittering
And squirming in the silt.
He pauses to pick a bouquet

Of seaweed for the young girls on the dock.
Rising he bursts the surface of this poem.
He listens for shouts.
He hears only the night
And a buoy sloshing in the blue.

Tornado

Four farms over it looked like a braid of black hemp
I could pull and make the whole sky ring.
And I remember there falling to earth that night
The broken slats of a barn, baling wire, straw and hay,
And one black leather Bible with a broken spine.

I think of the bulls my father slaughtered every August,
How he would pull out of that rank sea
A pair of collapsed lungs, stomach,
Eight bushels of gleaming rope he called intestines,
And one bucket of parts he could never name.

In the dream that keeps coming back in the shape
Of a barn, my father has just drained
His last bull. Outside it is raining harder
Than I've ever seen, and the sky is about to step down
On one leg. And all through the barn,
As high as the loft, the smell of blood and hay.
All night, as long as the dream holds,
He keeps turning the thick slab of soap over and over,
Building the lather up like clouds in his hands.

Ruth

WHY do they break all those bottles?" says Ruth. "Having fun's one thing, but who needs that stuff? God! It's—littering." Her words slip through the dry, steady thunder of rock'n'roll and that fluid, bantering noise of voices in a crowd. She sits between Eleanor and me on the curb, her thin knees spread slightly, her hands centered above them to cup a brown, stubby beer bottle.

Ruth is an Athabaskan Indian, but her flat, small-featured face always looks Eskimo to me. It is a pale, bas-relief face, not yet middle-aged, its delicate sculpture darkened by the quick angles of her eyes. Her hair is glossy and black, coarse, marked with faint brown highlights like striations on dark stone. But today—the 4th of July in Seward, Alaska—her hair is barely visible, pulled back from her face into a ponytail, then covered with a red bandanna kerchief so that only wisps and hairline show. Like a set of mismatched triplets, Eleanor and I are also wearing bandannas. Each of us is in jeans. We lift and turn our heads in unison too, sedate as tennis spectators watching two more brown bottles arc slowly through the air, then explode in silent splinters on a square of pavement.

"Two dead Indians!"

The shout is clear—high-pitched and boyish, coming from somewhere behind us and to the left. Ruth's head dips, her thin shoulders pivot toward the sound. "Bull----" she hisses. "You can't kill 'em off so easy as that."

"It's getting wild," Eleanor says. She drinks from her beer, then touches her mouth and chin delicately with a kleenex, so that small red marks come away on the tissue.

Today, I am thinking, is surely the biggest holiday of this swollen Pipeline summer, 1975. And until now, I've only seen Seward in its ordinary state—which is peaceful and sleepy, almost elegiac, slow and tranquil and nostalgically old-fashioned as any storybook city. In fact, I usually think of the town as a down-at-heel Land of Counterpane, nestled carelessly at the base of these fat mountains like a toy city filling the lap of some huge, dozing child. But perhaps Robert Louis Stevenson was "a romantic," as someone told me once; and my maternal, summer-tourist's appropriation of his verse *Garden* image may be no more applicable to the real Seward than is this wild and summery day.

Beside me, Ruth's weight shifts. She is sipping at her beer, and I decide that today in Seward is distinctly different: my metaphoric child seems awake and angry, about to have a tantrum. Even the sunny perfection of the weather has thickened into an intense, bright heat that shimmers and pulses, pushes against my flesh, surging like the crowd after the Independence Day parade.

The footrace up and down Mount Marathon has ended, but we watch a late finisher—a young female—jog a path through the throngs of people in the street. Her cheeks are flushed under their tan, her chest heaves for breath, and the sides and backs of her legs and track pants are covered with a thin coating of rusty earth. Her hair is damp and matted too, and one elbow looks bloody. A cloth square bearing the number 8 flutters on the back of her t-shirt, and a few hoots, then scatterings of applause break out in the crowd. Ruth, Eleanor, and I clap loudly. Someone whoops, and there is a shout of: "Good goin', man!"

"Man—?" says Eleanor to no one in particular, and we hear a ripple of laughter in the crowd. The runner nods, gives us all a tired and slow stretching of her lips—almost a smile—and waves.

Downhill, young boys tear apart an abandoned parade float. They wrap themselves in crepe paper streamers, light firecrackers and toss cherry bombs onto the newly-exposed, skeletal base of the truckbed. Two of them pitch more beer bottles. Ruth begins to remove her sweatshirt, and music from a loud-speaker at the foot of the hilly street blares and thumps a new tune into the air, syncopating rhythms within the chaos of noise and heat. Snake dancers thread their way around the floats, avoiding the boys, moving clumsily between the crush of street vendors and spectators.

"Look at those hippies!" Ruth half stands and points, flapping her sweatshirt toward the snake dancers. A long-haired couple appear to be copulating in the center of a circle now formed by the dancers. Eleanor covers her mouth with both small hands. Her face muscles are contracting and one eyelid twitches. "Yuk!" she says.

I probably look uncomfortable too, I think. We three are "of an age," as my Grandma used to say, and it is not the correct one for this day or this crowd. Our birthdays, totalled, would number well over one hundred years and, thinking of that, I shiver a little.

"God," says Ruth, as if reading my thoughts. "All this—I feel like an old lady." She places her bottle on the pavement between her tennis shoes.

"You—" Eleanor says with a snort. "I'm thirty-six next week," and she brushes, swats at a mosquito, but misses. Ruth lifts her beer again and sips.

A slender, barely-mature boy in mountaineer boots has climbed the brick and stone front of a bar and hangs from an over-sized neon U, his knees glinting white in the sun. He spreads his arms, dips and lifts his head like a circus acrobat. Whimsically shabby and shaggy young people gather below him to applaud, laugh, shout encouragement. A blond, bearded boy with a kinky ponytail waves his t-shirt, thumps his bare chest, yodels, then yells: "Hang in there, Tarzan!"

On the sidewalk across from us, a fist-fight has broken out. A barefoot girl dressed in the ankle-length tatters of a beautiful quilted skirt stands behind the fighters, vomiting slowly onto the cement. Ruth points again, and the couple at the center of the snake dancers descends toward the pavement, moving at an angle and almost in slow motion to disappear from our view.

"Lord," I say. "I had no idea it would get like this."

Eleanor giggles and leans across Ruth to pinch my shoulder. "Not like old Fairbanks, huh?" For nearly four years, she and Bernie—my husband Ed's younger brother—have been trying to persuade Ed, the kids, and me to sell our home in Fairbanks and move to Anchorage.

"Cripes, Eleanor, not like Anchorage either," says Ruth. She and Eleanor are long-time neighbors there. "Somebody's gonna get hurt!" As if in answer, another beer bottle arcs, then splinters in the street just two feet in front of us.

We are all standing now. "Maybe we should leave," I say.

"They're trying to tell us something!" giggles Eleanor.

"Leave! Not yet," says Ruth. "God, I can't be so old and square to have to leave!" She winks at me. "Just think. Michael told me to wear a dress here when I asked him! A dress!" She pulls her face into a shape that seems to intend an imitation of Michael, who is her second husband, the father of the two youngest of her five children. "Can't you just see me, in this crowd? Whenever I ask him what to wear, he says, 'A dress.' And heels. He loves for me to wear heels. Wouldn't I stand out here, in my taffeta and spikies? Laa-de-daa!"

We all giggle and butt shoulders like schoolgirls, but I am beginning to long for the safety of our tent (Ed's and mine, for we are vacationing without the kids for once) pitched beside Eleanor and Bernie's travel trailer, a mile or so below us on the beach shingle. As we re-settle on the curb, I notice that I am the only one of the three of us to have carried a purse. (A purse!) And I am suddenly aware of my own dizziness, a heady combination of mid-day heat and beer.

"Men can be so damn strange," says Ruth.

"Especially husbands," I say. "They're so inconsistent sometimes." I hear the hiss of my own slurred S's and think self-consciously again of my purse—and of the impact of this heat and the beer. I wonder if Ruth and Eleanor are feeling as disoriented as I am.

"Oh, I never ask Bernie *a thing* anymore," says Eleanor pedantically. She shifts her fair Botticellian flesh on the curb. And it occurs to me suddenly that her innocent pink body seems to have been shaped by that same intellectual virginity, the same childishly frank and simple process that usually builds her thoughts. I've always felt a certain affinity for physiognomy, I decide beerily, and not much of what I've observed of human behavior in my thirty-five years has shaken this.

Eleanor is continuing, her voice taking on a certain stylization, a faintly contrived but thoroughly familiar lilt. "Not thing one do I ask. Half the time he's traveling anyhow, for the firm. Just gone. But goo-bye, Bernie; hello, freedom. That's my motto now. That's why it's so great to have this dealership. Income! With your own income, you girls could do just what you please, too!" Eleanor pulls off her yellow silk bandanna. She shakes her head dramatically and pats at the sudden fluff of red curls with one small, dimpled child's hand.

"God, it's getting hot here," I say, dreading the possibility that Eleanor, recent convert to the joys of home-cleansing-aid sales, will again begin a monologue of financial theory. This morning's parade was punctuated by Eleanor's lectures on the free enterprise system.

Beside me, Ruth's shoulders draw up stiffly. "Well, I've had income and no income, Eleanor. But the world never changed any on my accounts. Not the women in it. Not the men in it either. Sure as hell not Michael." She sniffs audibly. "I mean, God, Eleanor. That's what there is about Michael, you know? Or your Bernie. That he's no feather to the wind."

"Oh, you," says Eleanor.

But Ruth's voice is continuing, careless but certain, I think, like the small sailboat I can see above the heads of the crowd, skimming the white-spangled surface of Resurrection Bay as I sip from my lukewarm beer and cradle my purse between my hiking shoes. "It's like I told Tessie-my-daughter. Be a good wife, try to be a good person. It means alot, sure. But, hell, life's not one simple thing. Freedom?" Ruth shakes her head. "I don't mean no damn stuff about incomes."

I know that Ruth's oldest child is nineteen and a young bride moved recently to Valdez, the summer's most apparent boomtown. "How's Tessie doing?" I ask, peeling at the label on my bottle.

"Well, she's been so lonely," Ruth says. She pats my knee, then lifts her beer and sips. "No job yet. She thinks maybe she's pregnant, too. Bill works those double shifts, he's out of town alot, and she hasn't got *any* friends there. Damn. That damn Pipeline. Big money but bad news." Ruth has exhaled, elbowing Eleanor on the word money. "So I told Tessie, there's no need to be—you know—a martyr. Don't hang around the place sniveling. Nothing like that. Just go out yourself sometimes, girl. Alone if you need to. Freedom, Eleanor?" Ruth winks at Eleanor (who sniffs loudly) then nods to me. "Go to a movie. Or go have a damn beer if you want it. That's what I told her. You just got to keep your own spirit up, you know. You're no good to nobody otherwise." Ruth shakes her head emphatically.

A police car inches through the crowd. The young bodies in the street part slowly—almost like a miracle on the Red Sea, I think—to permit its passage. As the car reaches us, I see that the two patrolmen are smiling, trying to stare straight ahead with faces that have already yielded to the impiety of those faint, testy grins. The young man hanging from the neon U yodels loudly, then waves to them. A beer bottle arcs and crashes against a rear fender of the patrol car, but the vehicle continues to roll steadily forward.

"My God," says Eleanor.

Ruth ignores all this. "Well, Tessie phoned me that she did it. Went out by herself. To a damn bar. First time ever. Bill was out of town again, so— That's about all there is there, Tessie says—bars. Anyhow, she sits down at a table, orders her a beer, and this girl comes right up to her. 'Do you have a pimp?' asks this girl. Bold like brass!" Ruth narrows her eyes, looks into my face. "Tessie gets mad. 'Hell, no!' she says to the girl. 'I'm no whore. I'm a nice girl. I'm married. I've got a mother and every-thing!'"

Eleanor grimaces, makes a sound between choking and a chuckle. I feel the small muscles at the corners of my mouth begin to ache.

Ruth closes her eyes, nods. "It's true. Tessie told me. The girl says, 'Well, I've got a mother, too!' This girl is kind of insulted, you know? Kind of mad. 'Besides, I just wanted to help you out, kid,' she tells Tessie. 'See, you can't work on your own here. These pimps get together. They'll find out, and they'll beat you up. I've seen girls beat pretty bad.' That's what she told Tessie! It's true! That's it! It made Tessie vomit. My Tessie. That's what she told me on the phone."

Eleanor shudders. "My God," I say.

"Isn't that terrible?" Ruth's pale face is spotted with color now. "They beat those poor girls up. Not that I can think much of those girls. But, God —that! Don't those girls have enough trouble?"

"God!" I say again, ignoring the repetitiousness of the word as I watch Eleanor squirm through what appears to be another shudder.

"But those girls do make a heck of a lot of money, Ruth," says Eleanor in a barely-recovered voice.

"They earn it!" Ruth's face is a solid, deep pink now. "And hell— what does that mean, Eleanor, anyway? Money—?"

We are all silent for a second. Then Ruth continues in a burst of words. "Money? It's—life, Eleanor, damn it. Not just money. Something inside. I don't admire them any, those girls. Hell, they're whores. But you can't hide your head from that stuff either. That's what I told Tessie. And how can *I* say anything against those girls, you know? Hell. Everybody has got to live in the world. But nobody's free just by money, Eleanor. Nobody.

"Like, last week?" Ruth's voice is urgent now. "I heard—my aunt, see? She's in the hospital, you know? Diphtheria is what they said. Diphtheria. Bet you two thought nobody got that, huh? Anymore? Well, you know, she's an old lady. An alcoholic. Had TB once. All that stuff." Ruth lifts and drops her shoulders philosophically. "Well, she grew up in a village. They didn't have diphtheria shots back in those days. She's an old lady anyhow, you know? Half dead, even before the diphtheria. One lung. And the first thing I think is, 'Damn! I don't want to go see her! I might get it!' She's in the Anchorage Native Hospital, you know?

"So, my father writes me: 'Go see her.' And I think again about getting diphtheria. Besides, I say to myself, I probably wouldn't see her if she was just here in town on a drunk. In Anchorage, I mean. But what do I do? I go. Of course—"

"Yes," says Eleanor, nodding.

"Well, she's—out of it, you know? Just barely awake. Hell. I don't even know whether she knew me." Ruth pats my knee again. "But I was glad I went. After. Of course—

"Because it was like maybe I owe it to her to go. To see the way she has been a person, you know? Still—It meant nothing. Just life, Eleanor. You got to take your own chances, sure. For yourself, yes! But remember other people do that too, maybe. That's freedom to me. But incomes? Money? Shit—"

Eleanor stands, dusts the seat of her jeans with one pink hand. Her face has a slight, pouty frown. "Oh, you!" she says to Ruth. A beer bottle dips past Eleanor, misses Ruth's head by a fraction of an inch, and shatters on the sidewalk behind us. We're all three on our feet now, and I think rather desperately of our three husbands, out together someplace in this crowd. "Let's go," I say. "Let's get out of here."

Ruth scratches a spot on her bandanna, as if the spot has been grazed by the bottle, though I know that it has not. She looks hard into my eyes, grins, shakes her head. "You go," she says. "If you want to. But remember, it's 4th of July!"

Placing her bottle carefully on the curb, Eleanor leans forward and claps both hands around another mosquito. But when she opens her hands, we see that the mosquito has survived in some small pocket of air caught between her palms. We watch its fragile, ugly form lift slowly and fly away.

GERALD CABLE

Ancient Forests
of the Near East

Straighten up, almost broke
my back—but I've flattened the springs
of a two-ton truck
with log-ends. It was only last night,
while the moon, her bones
poking through, held sway
in a wild corner
of the sky
and the stars
threw down their cards, that a fine chill
touched at the roots of my neck.

This year no scavenging hip-deep
in dead-white snow for twigs
and the short-ends of lumber, crusted
with icy leaves.
Right outside that window, which
that moth will never understand: tiers
of wood
stacked in long rows. Soon the stovepipe
in blossom
across the forests of Mohenjo-daro.

Mr. Pete Totten

Gray stubble, wisecrack light
in his eyes—in a hard-
sprung candywagon, washboard roads
at five A.M.—the clanging
of his gorgeous hangover.

We were following the last
log we'd chokered
down the steep skidtrail
to the landing at noon, when a
chewed-up sapling, bent flat

underneath sprang up
and smote Pete just under the brim
of his hardhat—
right between his
Irish eyes. I thought he'd kneel

in the dusty needles—here
in his hands all morning
already nursing the deep, tight
wedge of his brow.
Had his skull

been a bronze bell
the fallers up in the tall timber
would have laid aside
their chainsaws, listening . . .
I felt nothing

in my young smooth face
and leaped onto a stump, freshly cut
yellow as the sun
the wide rings for good years—
reveling in my ignorance.

The Illumination of George Jr.

He lost it one night
on that long stretch between Canby and Adin—
whose name is spelled-out
in white rocks
on the hillside. A can of beer
cooling his thighs
bullet-nosed forty-nine Ford.

The easy drift of eighty-five,
striped world
running beneath while he dozed
at the spoke of the wheel—and woke
in a blizzard of sparks,
the smell
steady grind of burnt maroon

as this, our good car of now wars
flipped to its roof
skimmed the asphalt, and then
rolled over five times
out through the starry jackpines.

Perfect letters tilted
high on the barren slope behind this town
with its three streets
lined in shade trees, and a cold,
silt-laden river. Its dying
hitch-hiker several years gone
when I saw George

on the third day, moving
lightly from the door
of his father's grease-pit garage,
softly among the blessings
of gutted mufflers, the worn-down prayers
of bald tires—
still alive, aching

in the quick new flower of his skin.

Highway 299

Along a backroad to Oregon, leaving
your car wavering and melting
in the sunlight, you climb a barbed-wire fence
and jump down into a field of rock
and sparse, pale grass
and begin to walk
as though pacing-off a certain distance
toward the farmstead that's
been deserted as far back as anyone
in Fall River Valley can remember.

A house of high ceilings
a screened-in porch—two stories with an attic
whose dusty windows face due south.
The square-headed nails rusted
in the rotted wood—the walls
let go, the joists and rafters, the tin roof
for counting rain
spilled down in a cloud of dust.
A gust of wind
would've been enough, the weight of snow
or starlight.

Tall poplars, planted for their shade
and the company of trees
stand out at the foot of a ridge
where the scrub-oak begins—
and an orchard ekes out
small, yellow apples for a hundred birds.

Bent and broken plowshares growing rust
in a patch of milkweed—
whatever they tried to grow
in this outcrop of lava
it wasn't just a matter of casting
out seed
and then leaning back for the harvest
moon to rise.

Now it's still another feeling
that begins when the foundations are opened
to the sun
and there's nowhere for the dead to live.
And when the smooth skin
of an apple the birds have forgotten
breaks in your teeth—
under the sweetness, a wild
bitter flavor, remote
as a country with no roads.

Jane Dreams

Standing behind him
hearing none of his words
reading only the turn of his head
the flashing torso
arms stroking thin air
like a swimmer sprinting toward a finish
line she sees him away now with every stroke
    just so everywhere she looks
    she sees men swimming in the direction
    of women away from women while women
    are treading water forgetting
    about rescues or going for the third time
    while the strongest find
    the right currents
    and without men
    or with them
    go with a second wind
she sees wind blowing their voices to Kansas
tree branches vaulting their own limbs
outstretching every word far back
in her mind she asks What force
do small breaths add to the wind
now she feels wind in a huge sail
it is pulling a ship she is riding
the prow

Bruise

Touching the bruise
on the inside of my thigh
the bruise like an illustration
of an iris bud ready to bloom
an iris like a phallus
touching it I hear again
the sound of your voice
how it goes like a stone
to the center of a pool

where it ripples
in that wet bruise for you and goes
as far away as the pulse
in the small of my ankles
as far away as the pulse
in the temple of my head

it makes rings
a stone's throw away
in the undulation of hands
wanting to be with you
all over and over again

taking throbs and bruises
of the mind far away
into that mystery of sleep
called the little death

I don't let the bruise rest
letting its colors go
the way of all flowers
but push it to keep it fresh

Codicil to a Will

It's raining and the apple tree
you planted, forgot, then left
as you left me,
has not rusted as you predicted.
It's topped and spreads to one white veil.
The grass you hated mowing
grows thicker in its shade
and I planted, myself,
the cottonwood tree I'd wanted
for years. It loves the rain.

The hearth you ignored warms this April
with ash logs brought by one who reads
aloud to me by its fire from Twain
and Marlowe. The Good Book, whose charity
taught you to begin everywhere
but home, I hardly remember.

The shower tiles you began to lay,
then rushed from to mend
other people's crises, are caulked.
No faucets drip
as though they were a plumber's wife.
The eyes, intense as knives,
yet smiling everywhere, you said,
are met now.

And though I remember the April
of my nineteenth year, how I spread
under you, warm and damp,
how I bore you a son and daughter,
and followed, a good Ruth,
everywhere you went,
I leave you now,
nothing, no good will.

I've topped myself carefully
without charity and stand alone.

And though it rains now,
the rain is gentle.
It forgets nothing,
neither does it forgive.
It is the growing season;
it merely falls.

Night Muse

I've always loved lies and fairytales.
Rapunzel was my childhood favorite, the granny
always there to watch her.

Years cloistered, only twice did I let down
my hair, meet a lover, escape the granny-
man I'd wed.

Now I'm down to stay,
but only so far, backstroking
as if on clouds around a tower.
My hair is down to stay;
it grows, too, under my arms,
the hair I hadn't seen
since I was thirteen:
gross and black, thicker
than any man's.
I flaunt it above my bright bikini.

And now it's coming,
a good sundown,
ink as night, seductive.
I let down my rope ladder hair
for myself in the dark
and go at a word.

Gone wild in the dark with blind men
some would say, save for one
who might see me, keep me with him
in woods seeing autumn come,
dry grasses curled like pubic hairs.

Let no man speak
unless he can swim
and swim deep.

I plan to go as far as the swamp
furred with moonlight,
find the clear stream
and float,
long hair meshing
like kelp to the sea.

DAVID STARK

This One's for Mae

ABOUT fifty or so young duffers were milling around the Hospitality Room as Bert brought back his scotch. He kept one hand free, as though ready to shake hands, and carried on his head thick white hair with only a patch or two of pink. His face was regular, slightly long of chin, as if it had been a pretty good face when he'd been a young duffer himself.

"Let's euchre this bunch," he said to Al, and a sound, half voice, half belch, growled up from the ascot around Al's throat.

"Euchre" was a word Bert used a lot, whether winning cribbage at fifty cents a game or trying to get the Rich Widow or the Blond Bombshell to move in with him and play house. Of course he never said "play house" to the Widow, who was a friend of his dead wife, for he had a hunch the phrase would intensify the giggle that was her defensive fort.

"What kind of woman is it when you ask her to move in and she doesn't say yes or no she just giggles?" he'd sometimes ask Al as he threw a trump.

"A woman who collects oriental furniture," Al would say, knowing if there was one thing Bert feared, it was merging Taiwan Tastes with his Provincial Oak.

But the Bombshell, Bert thought, was not like Kate or the Widow one bit. She was the only woman in Alpina to leave her career as a doctor's wife to audition for a beautician's job and get the part. When he was with her he felt she was the juniper berries he and Al had used to flavor the alcohol bought from the Capone gang in five gallon tins. By God, living with the Bombshell would be like living with Mae West, he sometimes thought, for when the Bombshell giggled, she jiggled just a little like Mae on top. Still it frightened him to think of containing her energy in his thin walled house, and he wondered how he'd greet Mary Wright, his neighbor, when she called to see if he'd survived the night.

There was a shout as a young Lion detached himself from the bar. His hair was shagged short over tiny ears, and he was an ex-fullback from Michigan State, come to Lions, Bert had told Al, as good works replaced exercise and his waist overflowed with fat. This young Lion was one of the young duffers Bert like to euchre best.

"Bert, Al . . ." the young Lion said, extending a paw of a hand; looking surprised, Bert thought, when he gave back as good as he got.

"Damn Bert, got a grip man. And Al, hell . . ." Bert watched as the young Lion stammered at Al, who held his finger to this throat and croaked right back.

"So Bert," the young Lion turned. "How's it been; boat doing all right?"

"Boat's fine," Bert said. "Put on a set of Hood sails before I went to Hawaii—like on that catamaran, the *Horizon*."

"The *Horizon*?" Wrinkles appeared on the young Lion's brow. "I thought you had a yawl?"

"I do," Bert said. "What I mean's the sails are cut like the *Horizon's* . . . and the reason I mention her is I got to take her helm from Maui to Molokai . . ." Bert felt pleased when the young Lion's mouth opened to take the bait—for the *Horizon* was the catamaran, featured in *Boating News*, which had sailed from San Francisco to Hawaii at an average 27 knots.

"Don't know whether you knew," Bert went on. "But I've just been to the Islands. Stopped off on Maui on the *Horizon*, part of the tour, and this young duffer who rowed us in tied us off to a tree—damndest looking tangle I ever saw. So I took it out and threw a bowline in; the bowline, you recall, is one hell of a knot."

As Bert talked he watched the young Lion's eyes wander to the ascot at the base of Al's neck. Beneath the ascot was a flap of skin, and beneath that the hole where they'd cut the voice box from Al's throat. Where the young Lion looked, Bert saw, the ascot had slipped, and a tiny spot of mucus dampened the blue and red paisley silk.

There was something close to revulsion in the young Lion's face—and it annoyed Bert a good bit. If anybody should be disgusted, he thought, it was he and Al—by God, Al'd had throat cancer, they'd both had kidney stones, Kate had gone senile then died of the Big C—these young duffers still had to go through all that.

"So I see him watching me retie it," he said, raising his voice. "And after a bit I see him go down with the captain to take a look. Comes time to get on board they sidle up to me like I'm some old fool, and say since I know knots, maybe I'd like to take the tiller for a spell. So by God, I did, skimmed her all the way to Molokai."

By the vigor that had come into the young Lion's nods, Bert knew he's euchred him as sure as he'd euchred Jack Taylor at cribbage using a pinocle deck. And a good thing to, for the officious fool would have launched into some smelly adventure he'd had aboard his damn powerboat. He watched curiously as the young Lion's ears seemed to retreat beneath his short, shagged hair, then turned to a muffled rasp beside him, like someone forcing air through a rusted duct. He watched Al's lips, after a moment turning back.

"Al thinks," he said, "that it's time we go get something to drink."

Bert left the young Lion nodding and they edged up to the crowd around the bar, eyeing young Lions from Claymore, Alpina, Grand Rapids and Battle Creek—all priming their brains with whisky so tomorrow they could deliver their checks to the Great Lakes Home for the Blind.

Most were in tailored suits and blow-dried hair—young, ambitious men—and Bert felt pleasure in contemplating the joys their ambition would pass up and leave out. Euchred, by God, he thought, remembering the Lion's regional last fall, when he and Al drank a gaggle of young duffers under by retiring to the sauna each hour to sweat out the booze. Talking about Mae West and *White Cargo* and how Mae had looked in *Diamond Lil*—they'd stopped talking to find the sun coming up and the room empty but for themselves; a bit drunk, but they'd euchred, by God, and they slipped down to the lake for a drink.

"Al, what you think," he said. "The Widow or the Bombshell?"

As usual, Al was vehement in his croak. "You take the Bombshell, you get the chance," he said. "The Widow, she's o.k., but she'll never peel you any grapes."

As he smiled Bert fingered the seams that formed around the edges of his mouth. Was it *White Cargo*, he wondered, or *Diamond Lil*. He remembered the scene: Mae draped across the lounger, cooled by a large woven fan, beside a man in a panama hat. She had arched, lifting her well favored chest, drawling in an insolent voice . . . "Honey, won't you please go peel me a grape . . ."

He was snapped back to the Hospitality room by a sharp clap on the back. Turning, he faced the jowly smile of Sam Barnes, in real estate from Clapton, with Seaver and Johnson, both owners of Grand Rapids furniture stores. All three men looked to have lost hair, and Bert noted the lank strands combed across the Seaver's bald pate.

"Bert, damn glad to see you . . ."

"Al . . ."

"So how are you old goats . . ."

Bert had one drink and then another before he felt his tolerance toward young duffers coming back. After all, he thought, watching light careen off Seaver's scalp, fellowship and a bit of good was what Lions was all about. He had another scotch and then one more. Then he told the one about the Italian gardeners who were laying turf and had to be reminded to keep the green side up.

As he finished he watched Al wheeze out of what was left of his big laugh, wiping his hand at the wet ascot on his neck. Goddamn this world, he thought; it had gotten Kate too, though she had a stroke or two and the depressions preceeding that. And he and the preacher had spread her ashes in grey swirling clouds behind the stern of the boat. No, it won't hold still, he thought, not even for Mae—and took another slug of whiskey to swish around his mouth and throat.

"Say, you fellows hear the one," he said, "about the Bishop who sends his best young priest up to Alaska. Well, after a month or so the Bishop is feeling pretty bad—see this young priest's his favorite and he gets to thinking he's done him a bit of dirt."

"So he comes into Point Barrow on the plane, and its windy and snowing and eighty below, and they take him by dog team to the rectory which is not much bigger than a hutch. Finally, he's inside trying to rub the cold out of his bones, and he says: 'Simon, my son, I did a horrible thing sending you to a place like this. Let me get you a transfer.'"

"Well, the Bishop looks up, and there's this stunned look on the young priest's face. 'Why there's no need Bishop,' the young priest gets out. 'I'm really quite comfortable here. You see I have my bible for comfort, and my rosary, and at night, well, if I'm depressed, I have a martini before I go to sleep.'"

"The Bishop looks around—the wind's howling, the furniture is old and worn, for the life of him he can't fathom how the young priest can stand the place. But he's a bit of a drinker so he brightens up."

"'Ah Simon,' he says. 'That does put a bit of light in my day. Do you suppose I might have a wee bit of a martini to warm me up?'"

"So the young priest, he nods, 'Why certainly Bishop,' and calls to the back of the house. 'Rosary,' he yells, 'Could you send the Martini sisters out here . . .'"

As the laughs came in, Bert counted them as a croupier counts chips. Thinking of Mae West, some kind of woman, in her eighties and still going strong. Like he and the Bombshell, she sixty, he seventy-three in the prime of life—still above, by God, to drop some jaws when tomorrow he slipped twenty thousand dollars into the fund for the Great Lakes Home for the Blind—two, three times what this bunch could make. "Bert," Clem Hodges had said, when he broached him at the Lion's Hatchery while dumping smolt into the lake—"Bert, for that kitchen what'll it take . . ." And then Clem'd handed him his personal check for that amount.

It's the Bombshell, he decided, thinking of the pained looks on Mary Wright's, his neighbors' faces. It's the Bombshell I want to move in. And

he leaned over to shout in Al's ear: "Al, you got any qui—neeene"—
which was Mae's line from *Diamond Lil*.

And as he looked away not hearing Al's croaked reply, he let the weight
of his decision pour like warm butter into his gut. Because ten years from
now he and Mae and the Bombshell, by God, could be down two tricks and
still euchre a roomful of young duffers like this.

RONALD SPATZ

Tricks of Finding Water

WHICH of her features attracts him? The sloping forehead? The protruding eyeridges? The boneless, distorted, yet sensual mouth? "Dearly beloved . . ." The congregation rises. The mysterious array of animal scents is announced and invited. "Dearly beloved . . ." He has found an echo in her. First one leg, then the other. But why the left hand? The congregation rises. They seem to look beyond the heirloom veil of brussels rose point lace at the vast stretches of vein. Yet who can describe the fresh tracks under the gown of ivory peau de soie with a cathedral-length train. The groom disguises his voice. "Dearly beloved . . ." Miss Barbara Joyce Markel, the maid of honor, stares at the altar decorated with two sprays of white peonies. Miss Julianne Katherine Sprinkler, Miss Marilyn Murray Heermann, Miss Erica Sue Bentham, all carry daisies. The congregation rises. Usher, Mr. Gary Willis Cooley stands tall. He once worked in a hospital as an orderly. And like a groomsman he searched under beds, brought some surprises. On Fridays he read the pathology reports. Miss Ruth Ann Toomey, who now sweats under her best man, Anthony Washington, in his basement apartment in Cedar Rapids, Iowa, was not above cosmetic surgery. The growth she developed, as a result, was benign. In those pages Mr. Cooley also probed the half-eaten carcasses. His erection, a dead giveaway. "Dearly beloved . . ." Mrs. Edward Magnus leans forward in her pew. Her ruffled avocado chiffon gown is very similar to the gown worn by Mrs. Joseph Orchmann, the aunt of the groom. Conspiciously the Rev. Martin William Trimble averts his eyes, and the Rev. Lawrence Robert Mitchell clears his throat. "Dearly beloved . . ." The congregation understands Rev. Mitchell perfectly. They know what he has in mind—rooted in deepest antiquity are the tricks of finding water. They have learned that silently following animals and birds will lead them to the mouths of underground reservoirs. Likewise, Rev. Mitchell's mouth is large, lips full, teeth polished and strong. He speaks of a seafaring town in the back of everyone's brain, where an enormous pool, not yet filled with water and flanked by bronze statues, is the place for posturing and singing; where the derelict streets recall a curious spinning behavior, a courtship procedure; where *this* man, and *this* woman, were carried over the threshold of pain, and were changed beyond recognition.

RONALD SPATZ

Kabob

IT IS ONLY an illusion this thing with thorns. Don't be fooled. Anyone can grow glands! "But this is not my house," Barb says, "understand?" Across the room the framed picture of Tex Ritter hangs crookedly. And on the other side of the duplex wall a sleeping veterinarian scratches his ass. What else is there to say? That she should move to Nebraska? That she should raise prairie dogs that bite? That her hair reeks of cigarette smoke? Can I say it with flowers? "We are in a web of inflammation," I explain. "We are at the rub of our blood." Yet there is neither form nor content here. How can I pretend that it doesn't matter? That her three foot long scar doesn't disgust me? At my left is emptiness. At my right an avocado tree looms. Where am I to turn? There is a knock at the door (the coarse grain has dulled decades). Barb questions with her knees: *What do you want:* The keyed-up reply: *Steinmann.* The bed creaks. The lock holds. Barb strains: "What do I do?"

Then again, Nebraska might be nice. Or maybe Kansas City. Or better still, travelling back and forth between the two. Maybe catch a Royals game. See a home run. See a shut-out. Anything is possible. The river that slides by Omaha is loaded with fish to throw back. A dropline will do. Everything's right there at the bottom waiting to be pulled in.

But current plans call for Steinmann who has his ear to the door, who recently had his hair cut and his beard trimmed, who has a billiard table in his basement, to take Barb to a beach in North Carolina. This is nothing to sneeze at. Wasn't it just yesterday that Philadelphia rang the Liberty Bell? That New York fired forty cannons? That Chicago's parade was seven miles long? So it's not hard to understand the endless orbits of the moon, the thumping at the door. And before it's all over they'll discover secret muscles, clams that hop and clams that swim, the enthusiasm of words. Is this a good time (to pop the question)?

"What do I do?"

"I don't mind perspiring," I continue. "I rather enjoy it."
"I can't," Barb says softly.

TIME FOR A KOBOB? (There's no telling.)

What we have here is a choice between Nebraska and Kansas City, and a dresser piled high with sunscreens. Not exactly a sprawling technology. But neither is it the haunt of crows and cuckolds.

Even so, it's a funny sort of thing. Carolina's ripple-marked mudflats have a humor all their own. The long and futile jokes are maculate, livid spots on a sea of back trouble. And like huge ripe rose hips as large as plums, the certainties of *that* person of *this* place are subsumed. After a time the helpless laughter gives way to great swells of extravagant joy. There is nothing to prevent sailing close to the wind, laden with treasure. But soon the wind dies and even the brightest fixed star fades, pirating the tempting prizes. The tide slips in. And swimming is a necessity.

For all Steinmann knows is, *is* that this is his house and the door is chained from the inside. He does not try to understand. He works his spatulate thumb against the chain. His white knuckles in conjunction with the moon brighten the evening.

"You don't know . . ." Barb says.

Tonight in Omaha a sniper has already killed three people. The police report that they cannot dislodge him before morning.

"This is painful," Barb says. "I love him."

And in such cases it may be said that ecstasy is a derangement of the nervous system. (Death is unequivocal.)

"What do I do?" Barb pleads.

I make no attempt to extricate myself, rather, I move to involve myself deeper. "Tell him," I say, "to come back later."

SHEILA NICKERSON

News from Nikolai

The news comes late from Nikolai;
A fire there has claimed three lives.
The land around is still.
Christmas has not come.
Between Farewell and Poorman
Seasons come in ragged clothes,
The beggar summer quietest of all.

Wiltshire in May:
An Idyl

For John Haines

Moon hangs in the apple tree,
A blossom of light.
Through the cottage windows
We watch. The land lies still
All the way to Avebury and beyond.
Stones have walked with sheep
Over the fields to listen.
The zodiac lies down,
A menagerie of stars
Masticating night.

Now is time to pass
From our small beds
In the glass house
Into the giant fields
To meet those herds—
To kneel at their sides
And learn the passage to solstice.

Mist rises from burial mounds.
It grows cold, still quieter.
Cows, called to their milking,
Arise, trample down daisies
Their dark way home.
Grass reassembles itself,
And the fence posts come back
Like messengers down from the hills.

from
Songs of the Pine-Wife

8

Where stairs lead to the stars
We hang our wash in salmonberries.
The laundry of green hills
Goes on forever.
Our line of patched belongings
Ripples once.
Clip them—pants and shirts and loves—
From ridge to ridge
And hang your hair and eyes
All stretched with wear
Across the constant green.
You will come forth
Laundered bright as pines,
Sharp needles in your mouth:
No need, sweet changeling, now,
For the chrysalis of clothes.

10

Down the trail from Dupont
Through skunk cabbage green
You come with the trout
Banging a silvery death:
Bells of tail and gill.

Through the trees,
A view of the channel:
The fleet scattered bright
Like scales scraped at the catch.

29

At low tide in the wetlands
Grass opens to wind:
Lichens cover the rocks
As barnacles do the crabs.
Small maps ride everywhere
Hiding the surface of things.

30

From warm caves of love
The sound of washing rain:
Before the last of dark you go
To hunt the marsh
For mallard, for teal.
The saltwater dawn opens a door
To the pulsing bed or migration.
The breast of the frozen grass
Bends to your boot,
Feathers part to the secret flesh.
In the empty space you leave,
Cold grows into the wetlands.
The shallows where your body slept
Fill up, white tracks,
With brackish tide:
The final black.

31

Healing after birth:
Clouds press.
The first snow falls.
Earth shrinks into itself.
A last insect beats against
My window: I can open no more.

41

Surely nothing will outlast
This storm: salt wind through wires
The cry of all our bones.
Caught gray between the sea and land
We straddle clouds of coast—
Each drop a ghost of thought conceived.
Amphibious, ambiguous
We creep with limbs we do not know
The slow geology of love.
Where roots take hold
We come, uncertain guests, each one.

Though teeth of caribou
Festoon your belt
And you have walked the tundra night
North to Nome through drunken forests
Falling into frost—
You join me in this anteroom
Of strange gnarled doors. Draw near
Before the opening,
My forester, my earth,
While sea walls tear.

Taking the
Night Trail

This is the kind
of night
the moist forest shadows
lift themselves, spread
and offer their thin fingers.

The moon roams
the treetops,
you shade your eyes.

A tree falls from its roots
stretching silently
into itself.

If your feet begin
to fade on the way
you're so much closer to home.

Fragment of a Legend

Midnight.
Lowtide moonlight
pulls at the long shore.
The sea woman takes me again
in her soft skin
smelling of kelp.

She beaches me
at the original village,
the one
way back there
where all paths
are used by my great ancestors,
rich clans of hemlock.

In their tribal houses
I am Guest of Honor.
Their gifts:
songs chanted in frail voices
that tell
their totems are filled with the wind forever.

Game

I am a small boy again
and my father wraps me in deerskin
and tells me to sleep
while they sit at the fire
and boast endless hunting tales.

My father once upon a time
shot an out-of-season deer.
Dragged it kicking, into a thicket
of brush, smashing its skull with rocks.
That deer wouldn't die, it just hung
out its tongue, rolled up its eyes,
and bleated
and bleated.

I dream of toy animals
you squeeze and they cry;
of hysterical children mutilating them.
I'm jolted awake to a rifle-crack;
I try to sit up
but only a deer cry
bleeds from my throat,
and the men stand around
laughing and elbowing each other.

The Man Who Loved Knots

Evenings, your back is thick with blood
where the sun has flogged you.
Black pools appear at your feet;

You step into them
with your luggage
full of bones,
knowing they are required
on this exodus.

As you slide downward
and find a perfect fit,
you close the skin
over your head,
and I begin to sew
the sutures you showed me.

Fertility Rite

You make your rounds again,
those full moons in your eyes
always tugging at my seas of blood.

You open your arms and draw me
onto your shores
and I drift into your skin.
You lock me in; this is
my asylum; this is

the time of season
we pace our floors
and claw our padded cell walls.

We throw ourselves
into the moon
and thrash and turn
our heads
from side to side,
like suffocating fish.

The tides swell in our rivers
till they're gorged as kelp bulbs.
Two tidal waves collide
and leave us barely
sensing we have drowned
and now float lifeless
in this lunar emptiness.

We sink vacantly
behind our darkening eyes,
absently surveying the damage.

Fever

BRAD lay on his back in the snow watching the large flakes fall downward into his face; he noticed that the flakes spun like tiny wheels just before they'd strike; the heaviness of the wet snow muffled the sounds around him, and the snow machine that sputtered ten feet from him sounded like it was a half mile away. He wished it were. It was the second time today that he'd been thrown from it. He sat up in the snow and looked dejectedly at the machine. It sat on the river bed fouling and surrounding willow thickets with its thick oil exhaust. It was a yellow, thick-set machine, heavy and powerful; on the back of it was a box where Brad carried his specimens and equipment. He got back to his feet and walked over to the machine and studied it. He had been a field biologist for a dozen years, but of all the various sorts of equipment he'd worked with he hated snow machines the most.

Carefully he remounted it and accelerated until he was cruising along slowly; the machine crawled along with difficulty in the wet snow and Brad had to wipe the slush away from his goggles repeatedly. Finally, approaching a red flag that thrust upwards from the thick river ice, he shut the machine off and went to work at the hole. Slowly he dragged a net out. He carefully attached a marker onto each living fish and dropped the dead ones in a sack. Looking up at the cloudy sky he thought how ironic this land was; yesterday it had been minus 38, now it was almost 20 above. As undependable as his snow machine.

Occasionally as he worked he stuffed his hands inside woolen mittens that had become fouled with fish slime weeks ago; the sharp pain in his hands from handling the net forced him to tuck each mittened hand under opposite arms; he jumped up and down to warm his feet for his snow machine boots had become soaked with sweat and had lost their insulative value. He wondered what an onlooker would think if they could see him —hands under arms jumping up and down on a frozen river. But he didn't have to worry about that; he was sixty-eight miles from the nearest village and seventy-five miles south of the Arctic Circle. At least he had privacy.

It was nearly dark as he drove the machine out of the river bed onto the main trail and headed for his cabin. He had covered his entire circuit of 50 miles today and was tired; before going to sleep he had to measure and preserve over 75 fish he carried with him. Also he had to treat his dog's sores which had resulted from a fight with a porcupine. The dog never seemed to learn about them and hated to be left behind in the mornings. As Brad approached the cabin he stopped the machine several hundred yards distant; the cabin, covered with a foot of fresh fallen snow, looked an archetypical wilderness sight. Yet Brad had the sensation that something was wrong. He turned the machine off and listened. As the roaring of the machine died away in his ears he could hear the flakes pattering to earth around him; removing his goggles he listened carefully. The dog wasn't around. At first he thought that it had found another porcupine and was hiding under the cabin with a nose full of quills. Yet that wasn't right, for even Brad's dog allowed himself several weeks of porcupine aversion before forgetting and tackling another one. Starting the machine Brad drove to the cabin, stopped, removed the fish from the machine and entered the cabin. He put the fish on the sink but didn't remove his mittens or parka; standing still he looked around; through the open door of the cabin he could hear the snow machine's engine cracking away as it cooled. He could hear nothing else.

He left the cabin and closed the door behind him. Behind the cabin he looked in the dog house, and it was empty. Taking his flashlight out he looked under the cabin, playing the beam from one foundation piling to the other. No dog. Backing out of the small entrance Brad felt his back ache; a day of net-pulling hadn't prepared him very well for looking for a dog who was so damned stupid it never learned to avoid porcupines. To hell with the dog. He pocketed the flashlight and was about ready to enter the cabin when he remembered he needed wood. He walked back to the wood pile under the eaves; as he returned with an armload he looked up to his left, and on the roof eight feet above the ground the dog lay frozen with a broken neck.

He had dropped the wood immediately and walked inside. He didn't need to look twice; the sudden painful death was frozen across the dog's features. He sat close to the wood stove and poured himself a whiskey. What in hell could have happened? He sipped and thought, yet didn't think. Putting the glass down he realized that he was sitting in a dark cabin beside a cold stove, fully clothed, but he remained seated. What in hell could have happened?

A bear?

Yet it was December, and all bears were in dens; occasionally, a stray would come out during warm spells, but he'd seen the work of marauding bears and they didn't place dogs they had killed carefully on roof tops with broken necks; also, a bear would have finished the job by getting into the cabin, or at least by trying to get into the cabin. No. Not bears.

He ran all the other resident mammals through his mind and came up zero. Not wolverine; not wolves; moose was ridiculous; marten were too small. Also, the dog couldn't have jumped to the top of the roof. Eighty pound mutts made poor second-story artists. He sipped the whiskey.

He didn't like what was left; not at all. He stood and lit two gas lights and then looked carefully around the cabin; his footprints were all there were on the floor. Everything appeared untouched; he had heard no planes that day. He had heard nothing. He turned to walk back outside but stopped just short of the door; he felt vulnerable walking outdoors now, but feeling absurd he swung the door open and walked out. Without looking at the dog he brought in a dozen loads of wood. Then he unloaded the snow machine, bringing his cross country skis into the cabin last, then shoving the door bolt home solidly. Using a bag of diesel fuel as starter, he had the stove going immediately. Slowly he removed his boots and started coffee water. The whiskey made him feel more optimistic. Maybe the damned fool dog had managed to get up there somehow.

He made himself two peanut butter and jelly sandwiches and noted that the fire hadn't been out too long as the bread was still soft. With a hot cup of coffee in front of him and one sandwich already eaten he re-created the dog's ascent to the roof: Somehow overcoming the soreness from his quill wounds he managed to leap to the top of the sauna and leaped across the seven foot gap to the cabin. Possibly the dog had seen a red squirrel robbing insulation from the cabin. The dog hated squirrels. Squinting into the gas light, he tried to remember if he had ever seen the dog jump seven feet. While eating a last bit of the sandwich he decided that's what happened; the dog had broken his neck jumping to the roof of the cabin.

Feeling warm from the food and drink he shook his head sadly, as he'd grown very fond of the dog in the four years that he had him, yet it had never been too bright a dog. He went to the corner of the cabin and hooked up the batteries in preparation for his afternoon call. As he waited for the room to warm before switching on the transceiver he looked around the inside of the cabin again, this time proudly. It was the most fully-equipped winter cabin he'd ever lived in; it had cost the taxpayers twelve thousand dollars to supply, and another eight thousand to fly everything in and construct. Still, these studies would set the project ahead five years. Professional researchers preferred the comfort of the office during the winter, hence a study like this had never been done.

He turned on the transceiver. Adjusting it, he expected the crackle of static but it was silent. He doublechecked everything, yet the set remained quiet. He knew nothing of transceivers. It seemed odd that it would pick this time to go haywire, as more than any other afternoon, he had wanted to talk to someone. He turned this set around and looked at it helplessly; it appeared normal and intact. His mind returned to the dog. Thoughtfully he pulled on a pair of boots and went back to the sauna. After pacing it off he estimated the distance between the sauna and cabin to be about 14 feet. It would have been impossible for the dog to reach the roof on its own power. Walking back to the door he hesitated before entering; turning he reached into the box of the snow machine and removed a worn, rusty shotgun. Bolting the door behind him he cracked the shotgun open, put a shell in, then propped it up in the corner near the sink.

He sat at the table and measured the fish. He took special care with each specimen as in doing so he could forget that someone or something had killed his dog. Usually he found the tedious job of working specimens the worst aspect of his work, but not tonight. Behind him his shortwave portable radio boomed out Beethoven, courtesy of Voice of America. As he finished the last fish he put them in a plastic sack then stored them in back of the snow machine. He sat back at the table; there was nothing to do now, and he didn't think he could sleep.

He went to the calendar and calculated that he'd gone five and a half weeks without a supply plane, and he especially looked forward to the plane due this Saturday. He would fly into town, wrap up a couple of days of laboratory and office work, then head south on the direct flight to New York for a science symposium. Then days in New York. He let go of the calendar and rubbed his hands together. He had been out here since early October, and was frankly tired of fishing and being cold and of driving the snowmobile. Saturday couldn't come too soon for him.

He allowed his mind to think about the dog again, yet still couldn't comprehend how it could have come to be on the roof. Catching himself bogging down in the subject he threw open the stove and stuffed another piece of wood in. He thought of what he'd do in New York. As usual half of his time would be taken with answering questions about living and working in the north: Jesus, it must be god-awful cold up there? You mean you actually work outside during the winter? Do they still live in igloos up there? I hear you can make 2,000 bucks a week up there. I hear hamburger costs fifteen bucks? Brad laughed, for they knew about as much of where he lived as he did of New York. In any case, he'd enjoy himself—concerts, museums, and hopefully very few stuffy seminars. All at government expense. Outside he heard a thud.

He was at the door with a shotgun before his mind informed him of what it was; he threw open the door and forty feet away stood a cow moose and her calf; seeing him there in the doorway, they bolted, parting the willows in the thickets with a concert of splintering and crashing. He closed the door, bolted it, and put the gun aside. Those moose had been in the vicinity for two weeks. He poured himself a whiskey, rummaged around in the kitchen drawer and removed a cigar. Sitting at the table he tuned the portable radio from station to station and band to band; finally he settled on revolutionary march music from Radio Peking. His gaze took in the transceiver; it was damned queer that it chose this day to not work. It was a three month old set and he had read in three trade journals they were the best available; it seemed unlikely that it would just go out by itself—a brand new set. He went over to it, removed the rear plate with a screwdriver and peered into it; a wonderland of circuits coiled around like silver and gold worms. Nothing seemed missing or broken. He examined the rear plate; on it was printed, "Do not remove."

He awoke the next morning shivering; the fire had died down to almost nothing; looking at his wrist watch he saw that he'd slept almost eight hours. His head ached; he had had too much whiskey; on the table sat the almost empty bottle. He closed his eyes in regret when he noticed the gas lights were still on; although it was still dark, and would be until almost eleven, he turned one of the lights off and sat down at the table. He remembered dreaming sometime in the night, and this was strange as Brad usually didn't remember dreams. Yet this dream seemed unusually powerful. In it he had been driving the snow machine, much too fast, towards the cabin; coming out from behind the cabin was the dog, bounding along and howling its usual chaotic greeting. Brad hadn't slowed the machine down, but blinked the light on and off at the dog, then stood up on the running boards and yelled, "Get out of the goddamn way, out of the way," at the dog, for it bounded heedlessly at the speeding snow machine. When Brad clamped the brake handle shut the machine didn't slow at all, rather it sped directly at the dog. In the dream it knocked the dog thirty feet snapping its neck and killing it instantly. In the dream he had tumbled over himself getting to the dog while screaming over and over, "Goddamn it, why didn't you get out of the way, why didn't you get . . ."

He opened the pantry and removed a dozen eggs. He had eaten peanut butter and jelly for three days in a row and decided to have something cooked for a change. Going outside he opened the meat box and was removing the bacon when he saw the fish in the rear of the snow machine. Cutting four thick slices of bacon and throwing them into the skillet he cursed himself for not doing the fish the night before. Perhaps the sight of the dog on the roof had shaken him more than he thought; now he would have to do them after breakfast. He brought the fish in to let them thaw, and while eating he listened to the news. Afterwards he set up the scale and equipment. He sat at the table and measured the fish. He took special care with each specimen and in doing it he could forget that someone or something had killed his dog. Usually he found the tedious job of working specimens the worst aspect of his work. It was fortunate that a weasel or marten hadn't pulled them from the machine during the night and scattered them all over. The partially frozen fish chilled his fingers, and he warmed them by holding his hands over the stove. Finishing the last one he took them outside and tossed the sack upon the roof, up there it would freeze solid and be safe from roaming animals. It was only then that he heard the ravens.

Two hawk-sized birds squatted beside the dog's carcass pecking away frozen chunks of it. Startled, they flew away. Repulsed by the ravens feeding on the dog, he walked in and got the shotgun. He put a half-dozen shells in his pocket. Walking back outside he saw both perched in a tree twenty yards away. They didn't fear him, as he was in the regular habit of feeding them left-over food scraps. The ravens clucked, anxious to bet back at the carcass. Quickly he shot the first one, and as the other fled vainly in a death panic, Brad reloaded and shot it. Now they lay quiet in the snow like glistening chunks of coal; he walked over to them and nudged each one with his foot. They wouldn't feed on the dog anymore.

He put the shotgun away and sat back at the table. He drummed on the top of it and shook his head as he recalled his supervisor insisting on the snow machine; Brad had told him they were no good; noisy, ate gallons of fuel, not dependable. Brad had almost demanded the study be done on skis, but no; the supervisor wanted his field biologists mechanized, ". . . could do twice the work, more efficient, and if you break a leg you can get home with the machine, but try skiing home under those conditions." To his supervisor, it was a simple and obvious decision.

Suddenly Brad felt overwhelmingly sad, but fought it down and quickly went to the sink and busied himself by putting bacon scraps into the frying pan with some stale bread. He took the pan full of scraps outside, went to a tree stump and left it there for the ravens. Returning he took out his record books and with his calculator worked on his data for several hours. Occasionally he'd check at the window to see if the ravens had come for the scraps, yet by midafternoon there was still no sign of them. Putting his data books and calculator away he opened a novel but before sitting down to read checked again for the ravens. The pan still lay on the tree stump, its contents now frozen solid. He set the book aside thinking that he'd bring the pan inside to let it thaw, then put it outside the next morning. He was returning to the cabin when he saw the dead ravens in the snow. He walked over to them; it was snowing hard now, and the flecks of fresh snow spotted the birds. He rubbed his hands over his forehead; a fear gripped him as he kicked one of the birds over and saw the blood soaked into the snow. He walked quietly to the cabin.

Sitting at the table he trembled; first it was the dog, now the ravens. He couldn't comprehend who or what would want to kill dumb animals for apparently no reason. He hadn't heard any shots. Brad got up and opened his shotgun to make sure it was loaded. It was now dark outside, yet he feared turning on the lights as he would be quite visible through the window. Filling the stove with wood he crawled into his sleeping bag and stared at the door. He felt that whatever had killed his dog and the ravens might soon try to kill him. He pulled the sleeping bag up to his chin and wished with all his strength it were Saturday; he didn't want to be alone anymore. He began to cry silently, and as he fell asleep he hoped there wouldn't be anymore horrible dreams like he had had the night before.

RICHARD DAUENHAUER

Driving in a Snowstorm, King Salmon to Naknek

We leave the things of earth
behind: the river bottom, alder,
willow, birch and evergreen

for white becoming white,
the road defined by weeds
like runway lights

brown against the snow
on either side; the car
hurtles like a float plane

on a lake of snow, a taxi
on the step of tires, rushing
almost weightless, to the point

where the white strip curls
upward: lift off, where the road
parts from snowbound earth.

Night Flight,
Fort Yukon—Fairbanks

Night flight,
Fort Yukon-Fairbanks;
to port, Orion
and the half-moon;
to starboard
northern lights;
the symmetry of dials
and moonbeams
reflected on the wing.
Below us, frozen lakes,
snow defined and countless,
thicker than the stars;
the Yukon Flats:
a milky way of snow
settled through the black
infinity of spruce.

Lukanin Beach I

But to you, O Lord, what can we offer?
What can we consecrate
to you who taught the creatures
how to hear?

This image of the Pribilofs:
late afternoon in fall
a fur seal pup
loping on the beach
at sunset,
brown on wet, black sand
then passing through the silver
glare on gray
like a black and silhouetted wick
on the lip of a stone lamp rolling ocean.

Your own of Your own: we offer you
this image, this perception
of our being there,
a seed of intersection
and its growth
to memory eternal.

Russian Easter, 1981

As if
these northern lights confirm
what the music tells us
circling the church
with the myrrh bearing women
on our three day journey
to the empty tomb:
"The angels in heaven
sing Thy resurrection,"
but we on earth
still await the news
beneath the physics
of solar flares and shock waves,
energy showers
sprinkling the earth—
      the earth still frozen,
      crunchy, where we meet it,
      thawing underfoot
      after equinox, after
      Passover, but still
      not fully released
      from the hold of death—
while songs and incense rise;
as if perhaps
from some angelic vista
this steam of candle flame
is some
human northern lights
rising from the earth,
a flowing glimmer in the vernal
almost-midnight dark.

The Sinh of Niguudzagha

NIGUUDZAGHA had been abroad since first light. He emerged silently from the stand of spruce and trudged along a small bridge of planks thrown down across the slough. The dark side of Graveyard Hill rose in front of him. Unhurriedly he climbed the long slanting path. His steps paused at intervals that he might rest and draw the sharp clean air deeply into his lungs. Strength flowed through his slender body and into the crevices of his brain. Here and there he stopped at a grave sunken beneath the grass, only its tilted wooden cross marking its presence. Names and images slipped through his mind, locking him so profoundly into the past that it startled him when he found he had reached the crest of the Hill. The oldest gravehouses had fallen into scatters of boards and glass. Only the sturdiest remained. One of these stood at the point of the Hill, its corrugated iron walls leaning out to the river. At the roofpeak was nailed a large oval mirror of a bureau, the once ornate walnut frame buffeted and bleached white by storms. The glass was still intact. It flashed above the village like a watchful eye.

Wild rosebushes grew here, and the dry blossoms clung to bare stems. Niguudzagha stood motionless. With a stubby thumb he rubbed a rose into his palm and scattered its dust out on the wind. Parting the grasses, he came down upon the brow of the dome of the place where no graves were. He waited against the stillness of the Hill, his eyes lifted to the eastern rim of earth along which the mountains crouched like dark sleeping animals.

No-oy thrust his burning face out of the dark descent beyond the mountains.

A column of mist poured down the river, whitely muffling its broad curve. Far out in the Kaiyuh, little creeks swarmed in the meadow like coiled snakes. A moose stood haunch-deep in a lake, his immense antlered bulk a still, black speck. The waterways were filled with the distantly shrill commotion of feeding birds. A flurry of pale wings shaped itself roughly into a ladder, drifted south, and faded into enormous stretches of sky.

No-oy slipped higher with the imperceptible wheel of earth. His first blaze struck across the mist and lighted Niguudzagha's thick white hair. Niguudzagha lowered himself stiffly into a bowl of tamped-down grass curtained by weeds that rattled sparse and faint in small gusts of wind. *No-oy* pressed heat through the heavy red plaid of his mackinaw and he held out his hands. His lips moved. Heat crept steadily into his flesh.

Dew lay on the bark and plants he had gathered and heaped loosely in the sack at his belt. The sack was worn and stained with juice. He had knotted it of string in squares to let the green creatures breathe. Gently he touched a leaf of dock, sensing through the paper-thin skin of his finger-tips the rushing life under its hairy surface. He sniffed the sharp scent and murmured a few words. Leaning forward in the dry nest, he tucked the sack under the weeds. Then he lay back and let the earth clasp his narrow bones.

He was the last medicine man.

Closing his eyes, he summoned *sinh*. After a time, *sinh* floated down to him. His vision subtly altered. Against the screen of his eyelids he saw the people coming out of their cabins to the river, tiny shapes in barest motion upon the fastnesses of the land. Their voices floated up, no louder than the piping of insects. He sent *sinh* wandering through Nulato village, and the faces passed before him with their secrets. Niguudzagha was the oldest among the people. There was nothing he did not know about them. In this was power, but he demanded nothing of it. All he desired had been given. He felt regret only that a portion was now lost to them of the ancient and harmonious balance between the worlds in which they moved.

Andrew's face came before him. His clear questioning gaze fixed itself upon Niguudzagha's. Andrew, first son of Big Mike. His death had come in the time of leaves falling. He had gone out to set net for dog salmon. His canoe overturned. His faint shouts were heard from the shore, and then was heard only the voice of the river. When his friends reached the strong middle current, he was gone.

The people grieved because Niguudzagha could not perform the cere-monies for Andrew as in old times. The priests had warned them that to summon and speak with the *yeega'* of the dead in that manner was an evil thing. But there was yet a more serious matter. Andrew had gone into strange places and his wife and children could not lay him in the family plot. They were terrified. His spirit was surely lost. They implored Niguudzagha to find it. Having foreseen, he acquiesced. He performed the rite in the silence and secrecy of night beneath the cold dark river.

He imparted these matters to Andrew in reassuring soft mutters of Athabaskan. Andrew's face withdrew. Niguudzagha knew with a rush of certainty that he had gone safely to his right place. His *yeega'* roamed tranquil in the other world, much like this one except that there, it was the time of big snow. About him, speaking familiarly, the animals and birds attended him. He was set free of the other spirits who prowled fearsomely upon the earth. A shadowy curtain had lifted from his senses, and he was one with the world above.

Creases of pleasure curved Niguudzagha's cheeks and he settled deep into the nest. His old clawlike hands clasped and loosened. He drifted slowly back to himself and was immediately seized by the warmth of *No-oy*. Looking up, he spoke into the great blazing eye: "Now it is made good."

Since his youth he had talked to *No-oy*. He was even then given over to the things of earth. In the days of *esnaih*, when the band followed the call of animals and birds and of the fish of the river, he left the other children playing and wandered in lone places. As his years increased, he passed hours considering the ways of the earth and creatures. When he tired, his mind emptied of all but the great land breathing about him. A day came when he realized he had been lying on the ground engaged in speech with an alder tree.

At this, Niguudzagha smiled, remembering that he had not feared that first messenger, who would be one of his familiars. After his first speech with the alder, he ate and drank nothing for three days and kept silence as men did before the hunt. In the woods, fasting and faint, he fell down and lay unconscious for unknown periods. He returned with a sense of having entered vast bright spaces beyond the world. He staggered when he stood. Incomprehensible words came from his lips. He began to fly out far above his mind, and crawling on his belly cried once to an unknown being: "Give me wisdom to counsel others!" When he emerged from the trance he did not know how he could have spoken so. It was the way elder persons talked.

Niguudzagha's mind flickered again to the people. Today they were in vital balance. Daily he assured himself of their well being, for they were surrounded by the *yeega'* of unseen creatures. The mysteries, he thought, were beyond the small comprehension of any man. At certain seasons the spirits were honored in ceremonies, by all the people gathered as one. He performed, along with *sinh* and the lesser guides, other rites too potent for the telling. He never spoke of them, and never uttered the names of *yeega'*.

The people were loath to speak of these matters of the spirit world to the *Gisakk* priests. It was bad luck. *Yeega'* would be angered. But they confided, a little at a time and under subtle questioning. "Over us all is the Master of the World. Everything in the world is by him," they said. "He care about our game and fish. A man has to be careful. If he step on his catch or dirty it, it don't look right. It's like we don't care."

"One should never offend the giver of food, the avenger of waste?" one of the Fathers had asked Niguudzagha long ago.

Niguudzagha told him, "If we mistreat *yeega'*, then when the people are hard up, all this would come back and we would know we are being punished."

"You believe in God, then," the Father said.

With reluctance, Niguudzagha replied, "There is some Being who look down on us and see what we do. He is every place, but he has no name."

Now he scratched his head with a feeling of helplessness. He was sorry he had revealed this knowledge belonging to the people. But in a way, the Father seemed like another medicine man. Except for one thing. Niguudzagha had a persistent sense that he and the Father were not considered equals. Father wore a certain manner of authority. This went with the giving of orders, Niguudzagha thought. And only the Being of no name gave orders to the people until *Gisakk* came among them. As to himself, he knew he had always lived in the presence of the Being. This mysterious perception had been infused into him by the incessant dreams.

Gaagateeya', his grandfather, had understood. Grandfather was full of years and well accustomed to dreaming. One day he looked into the boy's face with eyes curtained by a white film. "Ah, Kuskaga!" he exclaimed.

That was Niguudzagha's name then, a name that meant harpoon, for his parents had wished him to be keen and straight. The name had been worn by an ancestor deep in the past, when the people lived by the sea. Kuskaga held himself utterly still for long periods, in the manner of the harpoon, waiting for that creature which he saw coming toward him in the watery, shifting shapes of the dreams.

The filmed eyes of Gaagateeya' wavered and Kuskaga thought they could see his face only as a blur. "You visit with the trees," Gaagateeya' said.

"Yes, my grandfather."

"You talk to trees?"

Kuskaga shuffled his feet restlessly. "They talk too," he said.

"Ahhh, my youngest son." Grandfather's white look glided out and fixed upon the gleam of *No-oy*, dancing on the river. "You talk to any other?" The eyes shone purely, like dentalium shell.

"Many other." Kuskaga bent his head and studied the stones of the ground.

"Who?"

Hesitantly, "*Doyon . . . Nokinbaa . . . Ggaa . . . Dotson' . . .*"*

"Oho!" Grandfather said. "These you dream?"

"I don't know . . ." Kuskaga hesitated. "One time I talk to real *Dotson'* on a tree!"

"Oh, that fellow! What did he say?"

"He tell me I have to wait, that's all."

With a smile, Grandfather said, "You get scared and nervous, yah?"

"All the time," Kuskaga admitted.

Grandfather's eyes closed. After a while he said, "That's good." He pulled Kuskaga to his knee. "You have fourteen years now, isn't it? Always you wait for something and you wonder what is that thing. Now I tell you. You will be medicine man, I think."

Kuskaga's breath caught, and his mind circled among all he had seen and heard. At least he had received an answer to the endless puzzle of his mysterious actions. His chest tightened. "How can this be?"

"All these creatures are your helpers," Grandfather said. "They bring big message. First you will learn all about our people and the land we walk upon here. You will know animals and their *yeega'*. At a time when it is right, your *sinh* will come. When that happen, you will go far out of yourself and you will be medicine man. But you will learn more. You will know the secret language of *sinh*. You will make *yeega'* songs and sing to game and fish. Then you will pass under the river."

At this, Kuskaga shivered. He gasped, thinking: I dream too much. I have no strength. How can I do medicine man's work?

Grandfather smiled. His broad front teeth protruded, a wide space at each side like Beaver's. Kuskaga remembered with a shock that Grandfather was a medicine man of the old time. He had been named Gaagateeya' for Beaver, the builder. He passed under the river like Beaver.

Now Grandfather became animated. His voice came forth powerfully. "You will get strong and well, and you will lose fear. You will cure and counsel. All will come, if it is to be. It is a gift of the Being." His small bright face glowed toward his grandson.

Instantly Kuskaga knew Grandfather had heard his thought.

"I see you remember I make medicine before," Grandfather continued. "I just wait for you to get ready. I perceive much, youngest son."

Kuskaga stared at him. "Oh! You see with blind eyes?"

Gaagateeya' nodded. "Not just this place I see, but others. Where I may wish to be, I'm there." He raised his hand.

An exquisite pain flashed through Kuskaga's being. A breath of sudden wind stirred his hair. All about was a fluttering of wings and the raucous warning cries of *Dotson'*. A cloud drew across *No-oy*'s face. Two feral eyes glowed in the darkened air, and Kuskaga hid his face behind his arm.

He felt himself return from an infinite distance.

"You see?" Grandfather said.

*   *   *

Kuskaga entered another condition. His dreams began to shift and change. Sometimes he took the shape of *Doyon*, and grunting, clawed the earth in rage. Once he went into the body of *Nokinbaa* and saw tiny scurring voles and lemmings with such clarity that he felt an intense blood hunger.

He perceived ever more deeply the meanings of his calling. Constantly he was accompanied by the cries of birds and the shuffling whirr of their wings. He prowled for miles back into the empty tundra, acquiring knowledge of the spirit of the night and discerning the ways of its living things.

Gaagateeya' endlessly instructed his youngest son.

Kuskaga's face grew a solemnity that was transformed in rare moments by a great belly laugh that shook the length of his frame. He loomed skyward and his ebony eyes gazed down at Grandfather from his new height. The hollows between his ribs filled and he became lean and solid with muscle. The child's nervousness was replaced by a deepening serenity. He was nineteen when one day Gaagateeya' called him. Grandfather wore a look of pride that he quickly hid. His head came painfully erect between his crooked shoulders. "I call you youngest son no more," he said in the soft tones of Athabaskan.

Kuskaga squatted before him, his slim bronzed face intent. He fixed each detail of Grandfather's person solidly into his memory.

"Now I can teach you nothing."

"Ahhh," Kuskaga breathed.

"You must learn the rest of your part alone."

Kuskaga's *yeega'* was heavy. He stared at Grandfather's hands, lying idle on his thighs, and he laid his own big hand over them. He felt the small knobs grown upon the ends of the fingers with a thrill of regret mingled with tenderness. Standing, he opened his *yeega'* to the powerful current that passed from Grandfather's *yeega'* into him. In silence he turned and strode away on the boardwalk. He felt the eyes of pearl gleaming behind him.

            *   *   *

Only a few days later, in the early dusk of the month of freeze-up, Kuskaga sat on a log among dark spruce trees. Snow sifted lightly from their branches. The forest grew still, and the silence tensed all around. His nerves and muscles gathered and he quivered with anticipation.

There was a swift breath of wings upon his face.

And he passed profoundly into another place. He was almost dreaming, yet not wholly; it was more than dream: it was an endless thought in an absence of time, a slow flood carrying him to the center of existence. He flowed upon it, weightless.

The brown head appeared. An ivory disc of minute feathers lay flat around the immense yellow-moon eye with its fixed black pupil, staring past him. Now he glimpsed the beak, an ebony hook resting in the bronze breast overlaid with delicate creamy stripes blending into a body of dappled rust. Below, he saw the pale ruffled boots, and at last the merciless shining black talons, curled around a dead willow branch.

Suddenly the feathers rippled and stood out. The talons shifted. The intricate tail feathers quivered. The brown head turned full to him. The ear tufts lifted high over the eyes, the eyes that dilated to unbearable intensity.

Great Horned Owl was asking a question.

Will you choose? came the words into Kuskaga's mind.

His larynx bobbed wildly in his throat. His fingers groped forward and dabbed at the exquisite feathers of the breast. Owl sidled away on the branch.

"Tell Sinh. What do you want?" Again the deep voice filled Kuskaga's mind. His mouth was full of dryness and he swallowed again. He was made dumb by the hammering of his heart.

Ho-hohoo ho ho—Ho-hohoo ho ho. Often before, he had listened to the low call of Owl, but now his hearing had become painfully acute. The beak opened, and the hoots, pitched more loudly, hummed through him like the singing of a fine wire. The fierce yellow eyes flashed shut and open, and he saw their clean surfaces, flat as glass.

I call you Niguudzagha now? The voice was as sad as a mourning chant.

He perceived he had been in this place with Owl many times grieving for the past, for the future, of the people. With a flash of foreknowledge he envisioned all the smothered griefs of living. He endured upon his yeega' the weight of years falling with the force of a blow. It was too great. His tears fell, and he saw the wind spirit rising, the blowing snow.

Owl blinked rapidly. Take my name, Niguudzagha.

Ahhh. He had known these words by some means, unearthly it might be, in dreams or in another time. They were so familiar he had not recognized them for the words he had awaited all his life. There was an instant clamor or roaring, grunting and squawking from unseen presences all around. He shivered with the chill of their malice.

"Yes! It is my name. I claim it!"

As soon as he said the words, the din faded.

His head came up and he looked direct into the yellow eyes and he went closer, and closer, until he lay small and flat against Owl's enormous eye. He was plunged instantly into a vast and fiery brilliance. There came a rush more swift than wind. He entered the immense round darkness behind the eye of Owl.

He was naked in the place of no light, falling past the jagged walls of an *abyss. Lightning streaked around him. Talons lifted him high and laid him belly down on the wings of Owl. They spiralled up toward a far splash of light. It grew larger and there appeared two towering dark cliffs whose feet stood in a river beside the colossal bones of ancient animals. The cliffs moved rumbling toward each other. Owl swooped through the narrowing gap, and it crashed shut. A bellow of fury echoed from the river as they emerged into a grove of alders.*

Owl turned his head with a steady stare. There is the Woman, he muttered. She paced foward in a robe of feathers, gazing with a single eye of many flashing facets. In them was mirrored the dancing universe. Silently she offered him a basket glittering with gold and another, heaped with bitter bark. He grasped the basket of bark.

Smiling, the Woman thrust a harpoon straight through his heart, impaling him upon the back of Owl. The harpoon flew to his hand and he hurled it into the sky. Chanting in a new tongue, he flattened himself again upon Owl's mighty feathers, and everything fell away as they flew out over the cliffs of darkness.

His mind hummed: *Niguudzagha.* He was lying in a drift of snow. The dawn gaze of *No-oy* slanted through the spruces and found his eyes. He sat straight up. Sweat wadded his parka. "Medicine Man." Now he uttered the words, savoring their sound. Bending his knees, he stared meditatively at his boots. A set of deep scratches lay in the short dense reindeer hair of the calf of each boot.

And he remembered the flight.

He sat bemused. Gradually he was aware of an object lying beside him. Taking it up in delicate fingers, he blew away the dust of snow. It was only a small bundle. He held it, feeling for its *yeega'*. It was gentle, reassuring, and there was in it a true goodness. He opened the packet of pearly sealgut. It loosed familiar creatures' fur smells. Now that one was the fine curled feather of *Nokinbaa*, and here were two glassy feathers of *Dotson'*. These tufts were the stiff hairs of *Midziy*, the reindeer, plucked from his beard. And this was a piece of the white backbone of *Gaa*! Ahhh! This was the amulet of the creatures of his dreams!

"I am Niguudzagha," he shouted, jumping to his feet. He started to dance. He was surely going to burst right out of his body. Then he thought of Owl. There was the clear sense of his voice, coming again as it had in his dream. Or was it a dream?

This is your amulet. Great Horned Owl is your Sinh. You have taken his name. The splendid words rolled around him as a shower of snow fell on his hair and he saw the whipping shadows of rising wings.

*   *   *

Now Niguudzagha returned slowly from his reflections. His body lay flat and quiescent in the nest. His slitted eyes idly watched the play of *No-oy* who, halfway up the sky, flicked his fingers of light through the clouds. The shadow of a reed fell across Niguudzagha's face. After these many years he had acquired a resemblance of Owl. It was chiefly in the fierce gaze of his black eyes. The dense white brows protruded like ear tufts, although they grew long and he had to cut them with his knife. His head with its full shock of hair was shaped like the round feathered skull of Owl. His bones were fine and almost as fragile as Owl's, and his loose garments had the layered appearance of plumage.

Unsteadily he got to his feet and swayed until his balance returned. He yawned gustily and stretched his arms to the sky like curved wings. He inched down the crooked trail that clung to the face of the Hill, hooking his powerful toes like talons.

He could have made the descent in the dark.

*   *   *

"The shaman is a magician and medicine man; he is believed to cure, ... and to perform miracles ... beyond this, he is a psychopomp, and he may also be priest, mystic, and poet. ... He is the great specialist in the human soul; he alone 'sees' it, for he knows its 'form' and its destiny ... he is ... man's basic creative response to the presence of the mythic dimension ... the 'bright world.'"

Shamanism, Mircea Eliade

GLOSSARY:
No-oy—Sun
Sinh—spirit guide
yeega'—spirit
Gisakk—white man

*Wolverine ... Snowy Owl ... King Salmon ... Raven.

JOHN HAINES

If the Owl Calls Again

at dusk
from the island in the river,
and it's not too cold,

I'll wait for the moon
to rise,
then take wing and glide
to meet him.

We will not speak,
but hooded against the frost
soar above
the alder flats, searching
with tawny eyes.

And then we'll sit
in the shadowy spruce and
pick the bones
of careless mice,

while the long moon drifts
toward Asia
and the river mutters
in its icy bed.

And when morning climbs
the limbs
we'll part without a sound,

fulfilled, floating
homeward as the
cold world awakens.

Circles and Squares

So many painted boxes,
four walls, a roof, and a floor;
when you sit in their chairs
or lie in their beds,
the light of the sun goes out.

Ah, when everything was round:
The sky overhead, the sun
and the moon, galaxies whirling,
the wind in a turning cloud;
the wheel of the seasons rounding,
smoke and fire in a ring.

And the tipi sewn in a circle,
the cave a mouth blown hollow
in a skull of sand,
as the cliff swallow shapes
to its body a globe
of earth, saliva, and straw.

A square world can't be true,
not even a journey goes straight.
Bones are curved, and blood
travels a road that comes back
to that hill in my heart.

So many buried disasters
built squarely,
their cities were walls
underfoot or climbing.

My feeling for you
goes out and returns,
even the shot from a rifle
falls in an arc at last.

So many boxes; the windows
don't break soon enough,
and the doors never fail to shut.

The Stone Harp

A road deepening in the north,
strung with steel,
resonant in the winter evening,
as though the earth were a harp
soon to be struck.

As if a spade
rang in a rock chamber:

in the subterranean light,
glittering with mica
a figure like a tree turning to stone
stands on its charred roots
and tries to sing.

Now there is all this blood
flowing into the west,
ragged holes at the waterline of the sun—
that ship is sinking.

And the only poet is the wind,
a drifter
who walked in from the coast
with empty pockets.

He stands on the road
at evening, making a sound
like a stone harp
strummed
by a handful of leaves . . .

Fairbanks
Under the Solstice

Slowly, without sun, the day sinks
toward the close of December.
It is minus sixty degrees.

Over the sleeping houses a dense
fog rises—smoke from banked fires,
and the snowy breath of an abyss
through which the cold town
is perceptibly falling.

As if Death were a voice made visible,
with the power of illumination . . .

Now, in the white shadow
of those streets, ghostly newsboys
make their rounds, delivering
to the homes of those
who have died of the frost
word of the resurrection of Silence.

Listening in October

In the quiet house
a lamp is burning
where the book of autumn
lies open on a table.

There is tea with milk
in heavy mugs,
brown raisin cake, and thoughts
that stir the heart
with the promises of death.

We sit without words,
gazing past the limit
of fire into the towering
darkness . . .

There are silences so deep
you can hear
the journeys of the soul,
enormous footsteps
downward in a freezing earth.

On a Skull
Carved in Crystal

He would need the exact
knowledge of death
to be so clear in mind.

To see past death to the hard fate
of stars, by fire and frost;
the deepest diamond in its pit
of coal might shatter—
the only speech possible to stone.

Intelligence is what he finds,
gazing into rock as into water
at the same depth shining.

Bone-box filled with potential
shadow, no longer the head
of a man, not even his shapen skull,
but a changed and luminous thing.

Mirror, glazed forehead of snow;
holes for its eyes, to see
what the dead see dying:

a grain of ice in stellar
blackness, lighted
by a sun, distant within.

The Eye in the Rock

A high rock face above Flathead Lake,
turned east where the light
breaks at morning over the mountain.

An eye was painted here by men
before we came, part of an Indian face,
part of an earth
scratched and stained by our hands.

It is only rock, blue or green,
cloudy with lichen
changing in the waterlight.

Yet blood moves this rock,
seeping from the fissures;
the eye turned inwards, gazing back
into the shadowy grain,
as if the rock gave life.

And out of the fired mineral
comes these burned survivors,
sticks of the wasting dream:

thin red elk and rusty deer,
a few humped bison,
ciphers and circles without a name.

Not ice that fractures rock,
nor sunlight, nor the wind
gritty with sand has erased them.
They feed in their tall meadow,
cropping the lichen a thousand years.

Over the lake water comes this light
that has not changed,
the air we have always known . . .

They who believed that stone,
water and wind might be quickened
with a spirit like their own,
painted this eye that the rock might see.

The Head on the Table

The enormous head of a bison,
mineral-stained,
mottled with sand and rock flour,
lies cushioned on the museum table.

To be here in this bone room
under the soft thunder of traffic;
washed from the ice hills and blue muck,
skull and spine long since
changed to the fiber of stone.

One black, gleaming horn unswept
from the steep forehead,
eyelids sewn shut,
nostrils curled and withered.
The ear thinned down to a clay shell,

listening with the deep presence
of matter that does not die,
while the whole journey of beasts on earth
files without a sound
into the gloom of the catalogues.

The far tundra lying still,
transparent under glass and steel.
Evening of the explorer's lamp,
the wick turned down
in the clear fountain of oil.

In the shadow made there,
a rough blue tongue passes over teeth
stained by thirty thousand years
of swamp water and peat.

Driving Through Oregon
(December 1973)

New Year's Eve, and all through
the State of Oregon
we found the gas pumps dry,
the stalls shuttered, the vague
windmills of the shopping malls
stopped on the hour.

The homebound traffic thinned,
turning off by the roadside;
I lost count of abandoned cars.

This is the country we knew
before the cities came,
lighted by sun, moon, and stars,
the glare of a straying comet,
sparks from a hunting fire
flying in the prairie wind.

The long land darkens, houselights
wink green and gold,
more distant than the planets
in fields bound with invisible wire.

We will drive this road to the end,
another Sunday, another year;
past the rainy borders of Canada,
the wind-shorn taiga,
to the shore of the Great White Bear;

and stop there, stalled in a drift
by the last well
drained for a spittle of oil.

The driver sleeps, the passenger listens:
Tick, tick from the starlit engine,
snow beginning again,
deep in a continent vacant and dark.

Missoula in a Dusty Light

Walking home through the tall
Montana twilight,
leaves were moving in the gutters
and a little dust . . .

I saw beyond the roofs and chimneys
a cloud like a hill of smoke,
amber and dirty grey. And a wind
began from the street corners
and rutted alleys,
out of year-end gardens, weed lots
and trash bins;
        the yellow air
came full of specks and ash,
noiseless, crippled things that crashed
and flew again . . .
grit and the smell of rain.

Far up the leaf-blown street
a signal clanging,
as a train with a bell
and one withering deadlight went by,
grinding the rails
in a torn billow of steam.

And then a steady sound,
as if an army or a council,
long-skirted, sweeping the stone,
were gathering near;
disinherited and vengeful people,
scuffing their bootheels,
rolling tin cans before them.

And quieter still behind them
the voices of birds
and whispering brooms:
        "This land
has bitter roots, and seeds
that crack and spill in the wind . . ."

I halted under a blowing light
to listen, to see;
and it was the bleak Montana wind
sweeping the leaves and dust
along the street.

from The Writer as Alaskan

As D.H. LAWRENCE has told us, there is a "spirit of place." In any landscape or region on the map, there is a potential life to be lived. The place itself offers certain possibilities, and these, combined with the capacities of those who come there, produce after a while certain kinds of life. In human terms, these may be, among other things, religions, art forms, architecture, stories, and myths, and sometimes the absence of them. This is much clearer when we look at tribal societies that have survived with little change for centuries. But it may still be true for us, mobile, and in some ways innovative contemporary people that we are. Place makes people; in the end it makes everything. Strong efforts may be made to deny the place, to silence the authentic, but the spirit of things will break through that silence to speak, if necessary, in strained and deformed accents. William Carlos Williams, in his book, *In the American Grain*, attempted to define what he felt had gone wrong with America from the start—the inability or refusal to recognize what was actually under our feet, or in the air, and to live by that. Instead we fell back on the old names for things, familiar responses to whatever lay beyond our power to see. The meaning of what he found is still with us, as potent as ever.

What do we find here in Alaska? Something absolutely new in American experience. Though it resembles all previous encounters of a people with a new country, for Americans (the great majority of people in the United States and in Canada) it is profoundly new. If we wish to read of the North, not as sensation or bald new report, we must go to Scandinavian literature, to the Russians, or to some extent, to the Canadians. I have found it clearest and strongest in the writing of Norwegian and Swedish authors, in the books of Hamsun, Vesaas, Lagerlof, and others. Strange and exotic to the experience of a southerner: the brief, intense summers, the long, sunless winters. In Edwin Muir's account of his early years in the Orkney Islands, I recognized the North: the long shadows over the treeless islands, the barely setting sun of midsummer. My second summer in Alaska I sat on the porch of my cabin at Richardson in the evenings and read through *Kristin Lavransdatter*, Sigrid Undset's trilogy on life in medieval Norway. And there on the page was the North I was coming to know. The book and the round of the river below the house mingled, and my being there had that much more meaning for me. This is what real literature does, it seems to me; it enhances the place, the conditions under which we live, and we are more alive thereby. But there is little in English that carries the authentic mark of having been made in the North.

It is not only the land itself that faces us in the North today, as real as that is, but the entire drama of European life on this continent reenacted at a pace that leaves us stunned and gasping. The experience is hard to come to grips with; there are few names for it, and too many old responses. We see Alaska through clichés to save us from thinking: "The Last Frontier," "The Great Land." What do these really mean, aside from a great opportunity to grab? "North to the Future," that preposterous slogan once flaunted on the state auto license plates: the whole thing is a travel agent's invention. There is no place called Alaska, just as there is hardly anything today that can be identified as California. But of course there was, and is, such a place, though it can scarcely be found any longer for what we have done to it, and are beginning to do here. What I read about Alaska in magazines is for the most part the superficial message of the tourist—he who comes to gape, but not to understand.

How long might it take a people living here to be at home in their landscape and to produce from that experience things that could be recognized anywhere as literature of the first rank? Several hundred years? A few generations? We know from history how long a people have lived in a land and then found ways to express that living in song and other forms of art. Closeness is needed, long residence, intimacy of a sort that demands a certain daring and risk: a surrender, an abandonment, or just a sense of somehow being stuck with it. Whatever it is that is needed, it can't be merely willed. And much of what we say about it will be conditional; in the end it will depend on the right circumstances and on the genius of a few individuals who know what they want to do, and whose material and direction cannot be predicted. All we can do is to project a few apparent needs and conditions.

The Alaskan writer faces a double task: to see, to feel, and to interpret the place itself, and then to relate that experience to what he knows of the world at large. Not simply to describe the place and what is in it (though valuable, this has been done many times already); but to give this material a life in imagination, a vitality beyond mere appearances. This alone allows the place to be seen and felt by an audience whose members are everywhere. It is not, in the end, Alaska, a place where a few people can live in perpetual self-congratulation, but humankind we are talking about. What we do and say here touches everywhere the common lot of people.

The Alaskan writer faces an additional difficulty which is everywhere around us, and whose effect can be seen in much of the writing of today. The way we live nowadays seems intended to prevent closeness to anything outside this incubator world we have built around us. Within it, individuals face an increasingly impoverished inner world. It seems all too characteristic of us as a people that we tend to limit and confine ourselves, to specialize and restrict. We prefer anything to openness. The sort of intimacy, of being available to the land in Alaska, to the things it can reveal to one willing to stay, to observe and listen, this is prevented, or at least is blunted, by the life most people come here to live, a life no different than one they would live anywhere. It requires of them no change, but especially no inner change. The weather is colder, the days a little longer, or shorter, but life comes boxed in the same meager pattern. To one seeing it after some absence, it seems a strange and lonely place; it is as if here, finally the dream of frontier America must face itself. There is nowhere else to go, and it may be that deep down we are afraid that it is already a failure so enormous that we have no words for it. This furious industry over the face of the land is a distraction, and in the end it will hide nothing. If Alaska is the last frontier it may be because it represents the last full-scale attempt in North America to build a society worthy of human life, worthy of the claims made for America at the beginning. The weight of the past is heavy, and old habits hold on. The natives in Alaska have already formed themselves into "corporations." The name is significant in that it is really *business* that runs our lives, and we are all conscripts to a system that divides and demeans us.

To see what is here, right in front of us: nothing would seem easier or more obvious, yet few things are more difficult. There are unmistakable signs that something may be dying among us: that capacity to see the world, to recognize the "other" and admit it into our lives. Invisible walls shut us out, or shut us in, and we make them stronger and thicker by the day. This may sound entirely negative, but it is frankly what I read in much that is written today. The poet Robert Bly made the observation not long ago that what most poets write about these days is not what is out there in the world, but what is passing through their own heads, filled with shapes and designs already known. Moving from the city to the country, writing about fields and ponds and hayricks doesn't change anything, though it may be a gesture of sorts. Likewise, moving from the city "outside" to another city in Alaska isn't likely to change anything either. Something else is needed, a change of an entirely different kind, and this can take place only within the individual—but by implication it would also take place between the individual and his environment.

The world of the poet has shrunk many times since the days when

Wallace Stevens and William Carlos Williams took for their concern the whole of life, or at least the whole life of a place. The world with which the contemporary poet characteristically concerns himself or herself resembles the self-limited world of the adolescent. It is a deliberate limitation that comes, I believe from despair, as if the meaning of our situation, the weight of the disasters that threaten us, is so huge that we cannot find words for it, nor perhaps even emotions. Therefore we shrink, become deliberately small and trivial, and chatter about nothing at all, huddled like apes before a storm.

An original literature is possible in Alaska, but much is against it, everything perhaps except the place itself. There is the inevitable provinciality of a newly settled place, the self-protectiveness of unsure people who tend to feel threatened by anything "outside" and possibly superior to themselves. The Alaskan writer must learn to live with the knowledge that what he or she writes may be recognized by only a few people, and the better we write the fewer those few will be. In Alaska, as in our society generally, the average person just isn't listening, and probably doesn't care. This may be unpleasant, but it is true. Everyman has no longer a culture, but sports and entertainment. Money and power are the chief motives in American life, not decency and justice, nor humanistic values generally.

I realize that there is another side to this, and that is the obvious and willing care on the part of the groups and individuals to learn what the land can teach, and to live by that learning. Strong efforts are being made to rescue large areas of Alaska from the destruction inevitably following on the rapid settling of a land. Some of us, at least, are trying to change our way of living, to be more in accord with the realities that face us. These efforts matter, though they reflect the concern of relatively few people.

In January, 1976, I went on a 900 mile trip through interior and south central Alaska. In spite of the many gloomy reports being written at the time, I saw that the oil pipeline after all had not changed the land very much. The old impression of its vastness, and, in winter, at least, of the uninhabitability of much of it, is still there, and will be, I suspect for a long time to come. That big land out there abides, as always. Projects like Alyeska are not yet the ruin of Alaska. Away from cities, what impressed me most was how little the land has changed since I first saw it over thirty years ago. Works and days seem lost in that immensity, so much so that one feels a mixture of awe, gratitude, and a little fear: fear of what could happen if all restraint on settlement and development were removed.

We can hardly look to the arts for the specific answers to the difficulties that beset us, for they generally provide none. They can, however, reveal to us a range of possible human responses to life, show us what it is like to be alive now, feeling and thinking. And genuine literature shows, as only great writings and art do show, the significant shapes that lie behind appearances. We can learn from past and living examples, poets and writers whose work owes some authentic quality to the North. What does it mean to be in this place at this time? How does it relate to what is happening in the world elsewhere? It is no longer possible to live in Alaska, or anywhere else, and keep out the world. We are in it, for better or worse. One might make a categorical statement: no significant literature can be written now that does not include in its subject the human predicament everywhere.

Literature must embody some truth, in what is said and the way it is said, if it is to have any meaning for us now and in the future. And this is why, for Alaska, clichés about the "last frontier" will not do. The truth of our times, bitter and disheartening as it may turn out to be, must be faced. Honesty and imagination are needed. What counts finally in a work are not novel and interesting things, though these can be important, but the absolutely authentic. I think that there *is* a spirit of place, a presence asking to be expressed; and sometimes when we are lucky as writers, and quiet in a way few of us want to be anymore, a voice enters our own, becomes mingled with it, and we speak with a force and clarity not otherwise heard.

We live in a world, that great "other" made up of nature, the wilderness, the universe. At the same time we are compelled because we are human and vulnerable, to make for ourselves, in imagination and in fact, another world in which we can feel at home, yet not too far removed from that other. One of the functions of the writer, the poet, is to reconcile us to our lot; in the words of William Carlos Williams, "by metaphor to reconcile the people and the stones." To tell us a story in such a way that we become the characters in a tale we can believe in. Isn't this what writing, storytelling, and the arts generally are all about? The money making, the market, "success" and all the rest of it are beside the point, though they may seem important enough from time to time. Alaska needs a literature as a matter of practical necessity, of self-identification. "A culture without dreams is finished. It has nothing to motivate it."*

A literature is made of many things, not just a few outstanding names and works, and there is room for all kinds of writing. But what has most concerned me in this essay is that literature so distinctive that it belongs unmistakably to a certain place and yet speaks for all places. It ought to be a task of the Alaskan writer to understand this, and to seek to embody it in his or her work. Otherwise, what Alaska produces as literature may go on being notable for its hymns to Mount McKinley, dead odes to dead salmon, superficial accounts of "life on the last frontier," or finally, at best, very thin copies of the many poems and stories written anywhere in this country today. My concern is with the writer who wishes above all to come to terms in some way with the truth of our times. Everything tries to prevent this, to offer instead easy rewards for saying the obvious and already known. I suppose that what this means is that the writing, the best of it, should have some commitment beyond the private self. This seems not to be a time in which anyone has the right to expect a seriousness of the kind I am asking for, but anything less will not be enough.

We need to be as clear as possible about the world we live in, and to have some ideas about our place in it, to understand and to accept, if necessary, the limitations that living on a finite and exhaustible planet imposes on us. Perhaps here in Alaska is an opportunity to deepen that understanding. It is another *place*, where we can stand and see the world and ourselves. The literature that is to come will bear the mark of an urgency, a seriousness that recognizes the dangers and choices held out to us by our involvement with the earth. And it may now and then be possible to recover, in a new land, something of that first morning of existence, when we looked at the world and saw, without motives, how beautiful it is.

*Joseph Campbell, "Man and Myth" in *Voices and Visions*, ed. Sam Keen. New York: Harper and Row, 1974, p. 79.

Notes on the Writers

Edgar Anawrok is Inupiat Eskimo, from Unalakleet, on Norton Sound. His poetry has appeared in *New Letters* and in an anthology of Native American Poetry published by the Greenfield Review Press.

Jean Anderson is a sixteen-year resident of Alaska who teaches part-time for the University of Alaska, Fairbanks. Her poetry and fiction have appeared in *Orca, Harpoon, Permafrost, and Harpers*. Ms. Anderson is currently on the editorial board of Fireweed Press in Fairbanks.

Mary Baron graduated from the University of Michigan and now teaches at the University of Alaska in Fairbanks. *Letters for the New England Dead* was published by Godine Press in 1974, and in 1980 *Wheat Among Bones* was published by Sheep Meadow Press.

Gerald Cable lives in Fairbanks and is a graduate of the creative writing program at the University of Alaska. A winner of the Midnight Sun Writers' Contest, Mr. Cable has published his poems in *Permafrost, Silver Fish*, and other journals.

Ann Chandonnet grew up in Massachusetts, where she was born in 1943. She graduated from the University of Wisconsin and has lived in Alaska for ten years. Her books include *Incunabula* (Quixote Press, 1968), *The Wife & Other Poems* (Adams Press, 1977), *The Wife: Part 2* (Adams Press, 1979), *At the Fruit-Tree's Mossy Root* (Wings Press, 1980), and *Ptarmigan Valley* (The Lightning Tree Press, 1980).

Richard Dauenhauer was born and raised in Syracuse, New York, and has lived in Alaska since 1969. He holds degrees from Syracuse University, University of Texas, and the University of Wisconsin. Dr. Dauenhauer is currently Associate Professor of Humanities at Alaska Pacific University and, along with his wife, Nora, is active in research and publication of Tlingit oral literature and cross culture communication. His books include *Snow in May: An Anthology of Finnish Writing 1945-1972* (Farliegh Dickinson University Press, 1978) and *Glacier Bay Concerto* (Alaska Pacific University Press, 1980). In 1982, he was the poet laureate of Alaska.

Robert Davis is a Tlingit carver and artist who lives in Kake. He is a graduate of Sheldon Jackson College.

John Haines has published several books of poems including *Winter News* (Wesleyan University Press, 1966) *Twenty Poems* (Unicorn Press, 1971), *The Stone Harp* (Wesleyan University Press, 1971), *Leaves and Ashes* (Kayak Press, 1974), *Cicada* (Wesleyan University Press, 1977), *In a Dusty Light* (Graywolf Press, 1977), *News From the Glacier* (Wesleyan University Press, 1982). His prose includes *Living Off the Country* (University of Michigan Press, 1981), *Of Traps and Snares* (Dragon Press, 1981), and *Other Days* (Graywolf Press, 1982). Mr. Haines was born in Norfolk, Virginia, and beginning in 1947 homesteaded outside of Fairbanks for fifteen years.

Albert Haley moved to Anchorage in 1966. A graduate of Yale, Mr. Haley has published his fiction in such journals as *The New Yorker* and *The Atlantic Monthly*. In 1979, E. P. Dutton published his *Home Ground*.

Robert Hedin was born and raised in Minnesota and holds degrees from Luther College and the University of Alaska. His books include *Snow Country* (Copper Canyon Press, 1975), *At the Home-Altar* (Copper Canyon Press, 1978), and *County O* (Copper Canyon Press, 1984). A recipient of a National Endowment Fellowship for the Arts, Mr. Hedin has taught at Sheldon Jackson College, the Anchorage and Fairbanks campuses of the University of Alaska, and is currently poet-in-residence at Wake Forest University.

Lee Leonard was born in Middletown, New York, in 1945, and has lived in Fairbanks for several years. Mr. Leonard's stories have appeared in *Stand*, *Permafrost*, and other journals.

Tom Lowenstein has published several books of poems including *Booster* (The Many Press, 1977), *The Death of Mrs. Owl* (Anvil Press, 1977), and *Eskimo Poems From Canada & Greenland* (University of Pittsburgh Press, 1974) which was awarded the International Poetry Forum Award. Mr. Lowenstein is working on a book of histories from Point Hope to be published by the University of California Press.

Nancy McCleery has worked in the Alaska poetry-in-the-schools program and for the Anchorage Community College. Her poetry has appeared widely in journals and in 1981 Uintah Press published her *Night Muse*.

David McElroy was born in Wisconsin in 1941, and holds degrees from the universities of Minnesota, Montana, and Western Washington. He has worked as a smokejumper in Montana and Alaska, taught English in Guatemala, and flown as a pilot in Alaska for the past eight years. His poetry has appeared in a number of journals including *Antaeus*, *The Nation*, and *The Iowa Review*. A recipient of a National Endowment for the Arts Fellowship and a National Council on the Arts and Humanities Award, Mr. McElroy published a collection of poems entitled *Making It Simple* with Ecco Press, 1976.

John Morgan is co-director of the writing program at the University of Alaska, Fairbanks. Mr. Morgan's poems appear regularly in such journals as *Poetry*, *The New Yorker*, and *The American Poetry Review*. His first collection of poems entitled *The Bone-Duster* was published as part of the Quarterly Review of Literature's Poetry Series III.

Sheila Nickerson has been an Alaskan resident since 1971. A graduate of Bryn Mawr College and the Chapin School in New York, Ms. Nickerson has worked in the Alaskan poetry-in-the-schools program and was the 1980 poet laureate of Alaska. Her books include *Letter from Alaska and Other Poems* (Thorp Springs Press, 1972), *To The Waters and The Wild: Poems of Alaska* (Thorp Springs Press, 1975), *In Rooms of Falling Rain* (Thorp Springs Press, 1976), *Songs of the Pine-Wife* (Copper Canyon Press, 1980), and *Waiting for the News of Death* (Bits Press, 1981).

Ronald Spatz teaches in the English Department of the University of Alaska, Anchorage. A recipient of a National Endowment for the Arts Fellowship in fiction, Mr. Spatz has published his work in a number of journals including *Fiction* and *Panache*.

David Stark is co-director of the writing program at the University of Alaska, Fairbanks. Born and raised in California, Mr. Stark attended the University of California at Irvine and has lived in Alaska since 1971. His poetry and fiction have appeared in a number of journals including *Northwest Review*, *Carolina Quarterly*, *Southern Poetry Review*, and *Poetry Now*.

Mary TallMountain was born of the Demoski clan in Nulato and for thirty years worked in the financial district of San Francisco. Her poetry and fiction have appeared in over 100 journals, including *Calyx*, *Poetry Northwest*, *Northern Lights*, and *Shantih*.

Morgan Wills was born and raised in Fairbanks. A graduate of the writing program at the University of Alaska, Fairbanks, Ms. Wills has published her fiction in *Exile*, *Permafrost* and *The Webster Review*.

Irving Warner was born in Modesto, California, in 1941, and has been an Alaskan resident since 1964. Since graduation from the University of Alaska in 1972, Mr. Warner has been employed by the Alaskan Department of Fish and Game as a biologist. His articles have appeared in the *Kodiak Times*, *National Fisherman*, and *Alaska Magazine*. A book of short stories entitled *In The Islands of the Four Mountains* appeared in 1978.

Catherine Doss, the illustrator and calligrapher of the cover, grew up in California, and received a B.A. from Lewis and Clark College. She has lived and worked in Anchorage, Alaska for nine years. She is a printmaker, calligrapher, graphic designer, and fused glass artist. She recently received an Individual Artist Fellowship Grant from the Alaska State Council on the Arts.